"Reading *Unbroken* felt like sitting across from a dear friend who finally felt safe enough to tell her whole story—and in doing so, gave me permission to look at my own with more compassion. This book is so much more than a story of trauma—it's about healing, reclaiming your voice, and remembering that every part of you is worthy of love. If you've ever felt like you had to hide pieces of yourself to be accepted, this book will meet you exactly where you are—and remind you that you're not alone."
- Isabelle "Izzy" Atkinson, trauma-informed embodiment coach, podcast host, and breathwork facilitator

"Wonderfully raw and relatable. A real, honest account. Don't waste your time with other books that sell you smoke. This is the real fire, get into it, enjoy it, relate to it, feel it, let it move you, and then pass it on to a friend"
- Tommi Benni, author

"It is rare for a story so shockingly heartbreaking to be told with such warmth, passion, and honesty. This is a story of triumph and reclamation that I recommend to anyone. For survivors: Please read this and know you are not alone. For everyone: These stories are far more common than we think, and it's time to shine a light on them. Gabriella does this with strength and sass, courage and clarity. *Unbroken* is raw, real, and confronting yet told with a grace, wholeness, and love for life that can inspire us all."
- Ayesha Durrani, astrologer and founder of Oath Oracle

"A fierce and unforgettable memoir about what happens when the body remembers before the mind does—and what it takes to come home to yourself. Raw, unflinching, and unlike anything you've read before."
- Gina Gretta, author, SA survivor, and co-founder of Bunny Bunny, LLC

"A must-read for every yoga teacher, coach, or energetic healer who wants to be able to truly understand their trauma-affected audiences. *Unbroken* is a book about courage when faced with the evils of this world, leaving the reader feeling empowered and equipped to navigate their own life's traumas and adversities, no matter what they look like."
- Karen Stephen, financial coach and public speaker

"*Unbroken* is a redemption story for women and men everywhere who have felt crazy, unwell, unseen, and unheard. This book takes the reader on a quest of self-inquiry, empowering each of us to remember that we are stronger than we think and our pain doesn't define us."
- *Tia Ress, professional psychic and life coach*

"Gabriella wrote the story that I—and so many other survivors of abuse—have been searching for but could never find until now. Not only did I feel seen, understood, and held through her journey, but she offers it in a way that provides a real path forward—a template for healing that doesn't just speak to survivors, but empowers us. Whether you've experienced abuse yourself or simply want to witness one of the most courageous and inspirational journeys out there, this book will meet you exactly where you are. The medicine is deep. And it's real."
- *Zack Alexander, SA survivor, spiritual and leadership mentor*

"*Unbroken* is a book that speaks to the soul. It holds your hand and walks you through a journey of healing. It really shows you that you can overcome anything and be a beacon of hope for so many others. From pain to purpose ... a well-documented representation of waking up from your hidden pain and the confusion and messiness of healing ... and the beauty and light that can still come from it all. A must-read for anyone needing to know they're not alone."
- *Natalie Stavola, career and dating coach*

"Full of insight and truth, *Unbroken* offers the reader undeniably powerful tools to address deep trauma and heal integrally."
- *Danica Hennig, educator, support and education coordinator*

"*Unbroken* is an incredible survival story and beautifully written memoir of one woman's journey to uncovering and healing from sexual trauma and incest sexual abuse. It is the real-world pathway of what's required to heal from a trauma of this nature and finally start to feel safe and trust in the body that was taken away from you at a young age by those who were supposed to love and protect you the most. If you want to learn more about the pathway and process to healing sexual trauma and incest sexual abuse, whether you yourself are a survivor or you just want to learn more about the process to create deeper empathy and understanding of others who are, this book is a must-read!"
- *Jamie Rea, spiritual and transformation teacher*

"*Unbroken* is a difficult but wonderful expression of what healing actually looks like. From the start, this book challenges you to take up a role in your life you may not know is available. Unlike the rigidity of most self-help books, there are no ten-step processes to complete healing. It is a path with ups and downs. *Unbroken* is a book about the joy and pain of healing, leaving the reader feeling hope and strength to walk the path towards their own healing."
- *Tim Glowik, coach*

"This book stands as a profound testament to the strength of healing, transforming deep pain into undeniable power."
- *Christine Pieters, women's advocate*

"Raw, honest, and deeply moving, *Unbroken* is both a testimony and a torchlight. Gabriella's words hold up a mirror to the parts of us that ache to be seen—and invite us to return to ourselves with compassion."
- *Kimber Wigley, soul alignment and subconscious transformation coach*

"Gabriella takes the reader inside her experience with honesty, courage, and a rare ability to find light in even the heaviest moments. *Unbroken* is both a testimony of resilience and an invitation to heal."
- *Jennifer Lee, somatic healer, reiki master, trauma-informed coach*

UNBROKEN

UNBROKEN

HOW I REMEMBERED,
UNRAVELED, AND
RETURNED HOME TO MYSELF

GABRIELLA CACCIATORE

AWAKEN  VILLAGE
—— PRESS ——

This is a work of nonfiction. The events and conversations in this book have been set down to the best of the author's ability, although some names and details have been changed to protect the privacy of individuals.

The content of this book is for general instruction only. Each person's physical, emotional, and spiritual condition is unique. The instruction in this book is not intended to replace or interrupt the reader's relationship with a counselor, physician, or other mental health professional.

To contact the author or for permission requests, please visit:
www.gabriellacacciatore.com.

ISBN 978-1-957408-23-1 (paperback)
ISBN 978-1-957408-24-8 (ebook)
Library of Congress Control Number: 2025914038

Published by Awaken Village Press, Sioux Falls, SD
www.awakenvillagepress.com

To the girl who held it all in—
who smiled to survive and carried what no child should.
You weren't broken. You were right.
This book is for you.
You made it.
And I will never stop fighting for you.

PREFACE

I grew up in the suburbs of Massachusetts to an Italian Irish father and a Lebanese Greek mother. We were a lower middle-class family with little money, but, as my mother would tell it, we were "rich in love." I'm well traveled, college educated, and high achieving. I know what it's like to have money, and I know what it's like to be dirt poor and living out of a car. I am the type of person who does something when she says she's going to because I believe all we have in this life is our word. I truly believe you can do anything you set your mind to, and you will learn that about me through this book. I believe everything is a choice, and once you make those choices, it's your responsibility to see them through. I am not special. I've been on top of the world and to the pits of hell.

When I was twenty-five, my entire reality as I knew it crashed down upon me. I learned my whole life had been a lie, a trauma response due to childhood abuse by multiple relatives and their friends. I would later learn I had been a victim of a pedophile ring.

At the time I am writing this, I am only thirty-one, but the things I have gone through in this life alone feel comparable to someone of one hundred years. Yet the trauma, pain, and suffering I have not only endured but also transmuted are something I am truly proud of myself for. I have gone through things that cause many people to become drug addicts, homeless, or involved in unfortunate lines of work.

At times, my life feels like a paradox. I understand that multiple realities can be true at the same time. I had a traumatic childhood, but I also have amazing parents who love me. My story is just one example that sometimes things can be both; not everything is black or white, good or bad. All of the bad things that have happened to me have pushed me to become the best version of myself.

My story is tragic, but it's also absurd, funny, and deeply human. I use humor as a way to cope, not because I'm avoiding the pain, but because sometimes laughing is the only relief after so much crying. Everything in this world is about perception, and I choose to find the comedy in life. As you read this book, expect to laugh at things that shouldn't be funny and to feel things that seem impossible to hold together. That's what survival is: letting everything exist at once without apology.

I have tried to write this book many times and at very different points in my healing journey—even when the story hadn't truly begun yet. Usually, that took place in the bathtub, the only place my body was able to fully stay present. The past was unable to sneak into my body while I was submerged in the water. This is a common occurrence because water is grounding, and there is no choice but to be in your body and in the present moment with all senses ignited.

Thankfully, those early attempts never worked out because, up until recently, I wanted everyone else to feel the pain I was feeling too. I felt so alone in my pain, like I was drowning in a wave of mind, body, and soul discomfort. I felt that if people could understand me, maybe they could love me and see me the way my inner child wanted to be loved and seen. Looking back, I can see that I was trying to force myself to do something I knew I was meant to do, but it wasn't the right time.

Our culture often tells us, "Don't wait until you're ready; just do it now." Writing this book taught me that this statement isn't always true. The experience was profound in the context of my journey, but it took time. Revisiting what I went through often brought up challenging feelings of hopelessness, but still, I remained hopeful in my heart that I would eventually find a place of peace. I got to witness and honor myself in stages of my life and was consistently told that I would one day be able to tell my story without crying. I can proudly say that I can do that now. Thankfully, the book ultimately came from the version of me that understands that people don't need to hear all of the details of my trauma to have an understanding of it.

My intention in sharing my story is not to place fault or blame on any of the people in my life. The things I went through as a child are horrific, yet everything that has happened to me, whether "good" or "bad," has brought me to this place in my life, where I am happy, content, and proud of the person I have become and am becoming.

In telling my story, I've been applauded for speaking out. I've also been told that my openness and vulnerability were too triggering. I've gone from standing firm in my truth to hiding behind myself and trying to keep everyone else safe, a pattern that I learned from my abusers. I truly believe I have the ability to help a lot of people by offering a story that may feel tragic and relatable but is also very uplifting and hopeful.

Throughout my journey, I've had this dual awareness that even though I was suffering and in a lot of pain, someday I would be "better" and that there was a purpose behind all the pain I had endured.

Oftentimes, children being inappropriately touched by adults is swept under the rug because it's so uncomfortable to address. Even in my own life, I could sense how uncomfortable my story made others feel. Trust me, I get it. No one wants to talk about terrible things like abuse or incest. I understand the subject is touchy, but if you or someone you love is living in this reality, I pray you find a way to put your own discomfort aside for the sake of supporting yourself and others. Many people have similar experiences to what I've been through and without the level of support I've had. It's important to remind them that their stories are important and they deserve to be heard.

I understand people don't want to believe their loved ones are capable of cruel actions and that it's easier to claim the survivor is "making it up," but we as a collective must do better at facing these things together rather than making survivors feel like they have something to be ashamed of. It may seem as though there is "nothing" we can do to stop bad things from happening, but we can try to support those who experience abuse at a young age so they don't continue these unconscious patterns into their adult lives. Ancestral trauma is passed down from generation to generation, lingering until someone breaks the pattern. As a society, we must look this demon in the eye and try to stop this from happening to others. When I look back at my own story, I wonder if there might have been some way or resource to help me feel safe enough to speak up. Could doing so have prevented the assaults I faced later on as a teenager and adult?

Throughout this story, you might not want to believe some things are true. Unfortunately, they are, and similar things have most likely happened to someone you know. Maybe even someone you are close to. According to the National Center for PTSD, one in four girls and one in six boys are sexually abused by the age of eighteen.

Sexual abuse is a societal and energetic issue. Once you are a victim, you carry an energy inside you that other predators can feel. It's not something that one can rationally explain. It's like a parasite that lives inside of you. Predators know this energy. This is the exact reason why it is so important to take personal responsibility for your energy and heal yourself from the things you've been through; otherwise, it will continue to show up in your life. I experienced this in my waking life and saw it energetically in my body during my first ayahuasca ceremony. So much of our reality is affected by our energy and the energies we carry in our body from our past.

There are two roads to take if you're an abuse victim. You either bring something to light and fight against it to heal yourself, or you continue the cycle of abuse (whether toward others or yourself). And, whether you have experienced this type of trauma or not, you can still become aware of your own energy and how you are showing up in the world. We often hold guilt and shame for our past actions, punishing ourselves over and over again in new and different ways we might not notice in that moment, matching the energy of what we experienced in the past. Just as easily as we choose to hurt ourselves, we can offer ourselves forgiveness by sitting and honoring the pain, letting it move through us, and choosing to look at things differently to let go of what we once knew to be true and create a new story.

I hope this book helps others who may be fighting their own inner demons and takes the shame away so they can speak their truth and set themselves free because taking a look inside of ourselves is the path to freedom, liberation, and sovereignty. None of us is perfect; we all make mistakes and don't always show up as the best version of ourselves. I understand these are hard things to look at, but avoiding yourself and your truth is a quick pathway to pain.

This world isn't either/or; it's both/and. Energetic and tangible. Science and spirit. There are things we get right away and things that only make sense after time and experience. If you're reading this, give yourself permission to hold both. We have the power to forgive ourselves for anything; we hold the key to our own liberation and happiness.

My wish for you is that this book helps you see that healing is possible, and all the answers you seek are inside of you. Taking full control of your life can lead you to places you may have never imagined or that you imagined but didn't know could come true. The feelings you desire to feel may be on the other side of some deep and heavy healing work, but I can say with certainty that the work is worth it. You will feel good again—maybe for the first time in your life.

LETTER TO THE READER

If you're reading this, I want you to know something—really know it, not just in your head, but in your bones: I see you. I feel you. I know your pain. Maybe you're carrying memories so heavy they barely feel survivable. Maybe your mind is a battlefield, and there are days you honestly don't want to keep fighting. If you've ever wondered if what you feel is "normal" after everything you've been through, let me be the first to tell you that, yes, it is. If you've ever wanted it all to stop, if you've been swallowed by darkness, if you've thought, "I can't do this," you are not broken. You are human. And you are not alone.

When I first started to remember what happened to me, I needed someone to tell me that this wasn't the end of my story. I needed to know that the hell I was living through wasn't proof that I was damaged or weak or crazy; it was just evidence that my body and mind were doing whatever they had to do to keep me alive. You're allowed to feel lost, furious, empty, numb, enraged, or exhausted. None of that makes you bad or beyond hope. It makes you a survivor.

Here's the truth: The toolbox I built for myself didn't always work. Some days, nothing helped. The pain was unbearable, and there were times when I genuinely wanted to die. If that's where you are, I want you to know that I don't judge you for it. Those thoughts are a reaction to violation and trauma, especially when it's been done by people who were supposed to protect you. Your job isn't to be perfect or never to feel this way. Your job is to keep breathing, not give up on yourself, and let time and patience do their work.

Even now, all these years later, the old voices still show up sometimes, trying to drag me back to that edge. I don't fight them the way I used to. Now, I talk to them. I tell them I see them. I thank them for helping me survive. I let them know I'll keep them safe from now on. It's not about fixing yourself; it's about loving the parts that broke when nobody was there for you.

Please remember: If you need to put this book down, do it. If you need to skip a chapter, do it. This is your journey. Your safety and your nervous system come first. This book goes deep into childhood trauma, sexual abuse, PTSD, dissociation, and the mess of healing. It might activate or overwhelm you. That's okay. What matters is that you know this: Healing is possible. Survival is not the whole story. There is more life on the other side of this.

You are not alone. You are not crazy. And you don't have to carry this by yourself anymore. If you need to hear it from someone who's lived it, let me say it: I am so proud of you for still being here. There is a way through. And I'm walking it with you, page by page.

Gabriella

PART ONE

SAFETY & STABILIZATION

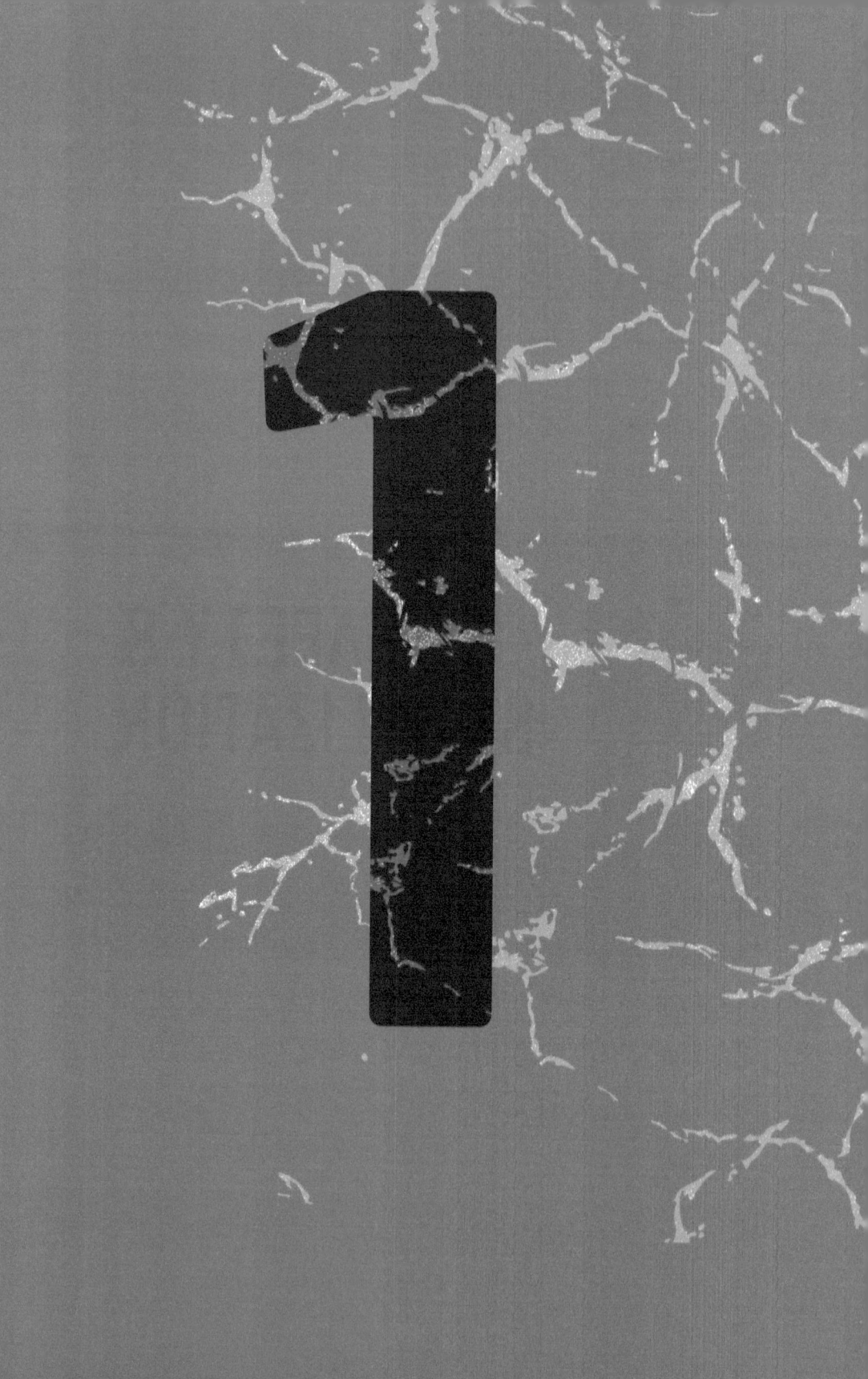

WHEN MY BODY SAID, "ENOUGH"

Looking back, I can see perfectly that the first thing I ever meditated on in my life was my own death. I didn't have it planned out or anything; I would have been cool with just about anything that would have taken me out with little to no pain. Drowning was off the table for me; that's one thing I knew for sure. I used to lie in bed and stare at the ceiling, thinking to myself how much better things would be if I could just leave this world. The afterlife is where I craved to be. There was no fantasy of graduations, weddings, children, the American dream—not for me. Just straight-up death.

I've always been a fan of God, growing up Catholic and all, so I knew there was no chance I'd take myself out by choice. I didn't want to go to hell—that would be worse than being here, or so I thought. So, instead of acting on these fantasies, I just let them be, circling in my head, watching the thoughts as they passed on through.

Let's go back to the morning of January 3, 2017. I was

twenty-five years old, off to one of my favorite places in the entire world: the gym. Specifically, the Boston Sports Club at 840 Winter Street in Waltham, Massachusetts. At this point in my life, this building was my sanctuary. Since I was fifteen, I had worked here, and so had my therapist. The physical therapist I was seeing for my neck and back pain was also in this building, and it was here that I met my current boyfriend.

I got to the gym, said hello to everyone as I always do, and hopped on the Stairmaster for some cardio. It's been four months since I've been able to lift heavy, thanks to the neck and back injury. I am bored and sick of the Stairmaster. On this day, I decided to bring *Healing Back Pain* by John Sarno, which my boyfriend gave me for Christmas.

"I don't want to upset you," he said when he gave it to me. "But I think the pain you're feeling is in your head. This book is supposed to help with pain by changing the way you think."

I, the hotheaded Italian-Irish-Lebanese-Greek girl, was not very happy about this statement, but I decided I would give it a shot nonetheless. After all, the physical therapy, massages, acupuncture, and neurologist were not helping at all.

So, there I was, climbing away on the Stairmaster and reading the first few pages of the book, thinking, *Wow! This sounds a lot like me!* Then came the kicker: Only a few pages in came the words that changed my life in a way I never thought possible.

It went something like this: A lot of the time, people with chronic pain were abused as children, and until they remember and face their trauma, the pain will continue. *Boom.* First memory, like a flash of lightning—at three years old, behind the shed in a pile of leaves, my Uncle Malcolm with his pants below his knees.

Panting on the Stairmaster, I looked at the clock and noted the time: 9:55 a.m.—the moment I realize my whole life was a lie. Everything I thought to be true of myself, my family, my world, shattered at the drop of a hat. I stepped off the machine and rushed out the door, fighting back tears. Then, getting to my car, I noticed something: The pain in my neck and back was gone. I called my boyfriend and started sobbing. This couldn't be real. My brain didn't want to believe it, but my body wasn't lying. With a single realization, months' worth of pain was released.

For as long as I could remember, I had lived with this aching feeling in my heart. I used to tell everyone that my heart hurt, and I didn't understand why. I was extremely anxious and high-achieving and would often have panic attacks or raging fits over small things that didn't really make sense given the situations I was in, but the feeling would take over my entire being. Several times over the course of my life, specifically at school and work, I had to call my dad to come calm me down during full-blown panic attacks. He would tell me that what I was worrying about wasn't that big of a deal, assuring me I would be okay, but my body did not agree, and I did not understand why.

Since the age of fourteen, I had been a fitness freak and absolutely loved the gym, which was like my safe haven and my stress relief. So I was thrilled to get a job at a luxury sports club in high school and continued to work there through college for the free membership.

After working there for a few years, the fitness manager

told me I'd make a great personal trainer and asked if I'd be open to getting my certification and working for him. He went on and on about how people were always watching me and asking about my workouts. I looked at him and laughed. *A personal trainer? Are you kidding me?* I was about to graduate early and get my marketing degree from the business school honors program. My parents weren't rich—I had to pay for it by myself—and I was supposed to be a businesswoman!

Regardless of my big ego and dreams of going into business, I considered what he had told me. I had nothing planned and decided maybe this guy was onto something. Why *couldn't* I study for this certification (while studying for my final semester of business school exams, like a psycho) and give this personal training thing a shot for six months while I figured out what I wanted to do? So that's what I did, and many meltdowns and one failed exam later, Gabriella Cacciatore officially became a NASM Certified Personal Trainer by the end of December 2012. That certification was harder than my four-year degree, an accomplishment I am still proud of to this day. That same month, I was put on medication for my newly diagnosed bipolar II, panic disorder, and anxiety disorder.

I had spent years upon years anxious and depressed, only to be met with comments like, "What do you have to feel depressed about? You're beautiful, smart, and you have a ton of friends and a boyfriend—you have everything going for you." This only led to more shame and self-hatred, added to the fact that I hated my body while people were now paying me because they wanted to look like me.

It was hard to wrap my head around this because, for my entire life, I had felt so uncomfortable in my body. (Yes, there is something to be said about being abused as a child and absolutely hating your body.) Mind you, I am five feet tall, fit, with a size G chest. It didn't matter what I looked like—whether I was a size 00 or 0, had abs, grew a big butt—I was never satisfied by the way I looked. It was a mindfuck.

With my new certification and business degree in hand, I decided to move out of the North End and back in with my parents in Waltham. I interviewed for a personal training position at the original Boston Sports Club and, shortly thereafter, started dating the fitness manager, who would later give me the book that brought back those life-changing childhood memories of mine. Lesson one of my adult life: Don't shit where you eat. We spent every waking hour together and were so in love—or so I thought. When we began dating, I told him I was dead set on moving to North Carolina (mind you, I knew no one there, but I *needed* to get away from Waltham at all costs). He agreed and, because I was making more money than him, I agreed to pay for whatever costs there were. I was young and naïve, but at twenty-three, I thought I knew it all.

Over the first six months, I quickly grew my business and realized I could make way more money doing this than working an office job in my twenties. My perfectionist, workaholic, overachieving tendencies took over. I worked endless hours, training people one-on-one and teaching up to twenty classes a week. I got certified in anything and everything, obsessed and unable to say no anytime a money-making opportunity presented itself. An extra class? Sure, I'll take it! More clients on the side? Great—the more money, the merrier! It didn't matter that I was already overworking myself. I'll never forget my therapist's face when she saw my agenda fully scheduled out from 6 a.m. to 8 p.m. It was very similar to the face she made when she heard I had saved five thousand dollars at age fifteen.

By 2015, at the age of twenty-three, I had created a six-figure business for myself. But I was burnt out. Plus, once I feel like I've mastered something, I am over it. When I was working toward the goal, it gave me purpose, adding value to my life in a world that seemed so meaningless. Now that I had achieved that goal, that purpose went away. I wanted out.

So, I went out looking for the next thing to bring me meaning. My boss boyfriend and I packed up all our things, said goodbye to our friends and family, and drove down to Raleigh, North Carolina. We rented a beautiful two-bedroom, two-bathroom apartment—heaven for the girl who had spent her entire life sharing one bathroom among five people. I got a job as a recruiter while he worked as a fitness manager at the gym. We made amazing new friends and were having the time of our lives. I only lasted two weeks at the job before I left crying—I knew I was never meant to be in an office—but all was well. He hired me as a trainer at his gym, and that burnt-out feeling quickly vanished as reality slapped me in the face. I came to the conclusion that it was better to do something I loved than suffer doing something I hated.

Now this is the most important part for me: Living in North Carolina made me so happy that for the first time in my entire life, I actually felt genuine joy. I will never forget driving in the back seat of an Uber with our new friends and turning to them to say, "Is this what happiness feels like?" I finally had a place that felt good to me, was with my future husband, and had money and amazing, supportive, loving friends. Life was good. But, as my therapist had warned me, geographical relocation was not the solution to an internal problem. *Oof.* And it definitely wasn't the solution for mine.

In 2015, when we drove back to Raleigh after spending Christmas in Massachusetts, something just didn't feel quite right to me. After hours of silence, my boyfriend finally told me he didn't know if he felt the same way about me anymore, explaining that he felt like less of a man with me because I made more money than he did and that he didn't know if he wanted to do this anymore. I couldn't believe it. This man, whom I spent every waking hour with, not parting even to shower, had now decided he was unsure about me? What the actual fuck was happening? Twenty-four-year-old me did not want this to be real.

On New Year's Eve, I was devastated when he went off somewhere with his friend and left me alone. The next day, I told him, "If you want to break the lease and move home, we can. But this is on you." So, that's what we did. We broke the lease, I packed up my car, and we both moved back to Massachusetts.

I was absolutely heartbroken. I had just lost not only the man I thought I was going to marry but also the little bit of happiness I finally felt about the life I was living. I was full of shame for my failed attempt at freedom, and all I wanted was to fucking die. The feeling was all too familiar to me.

I know you may wonder why I didn't just stay there if I was so happy. Well, at this point in my life, I didn't have the awareness that I could do things on my own. I believed I needed someone with me to do what I wanted; otherwise, it wasn't safe, or I was just incapable. So, by January 2016, I found myself at the beginning of my self-declared quarter-life crisis. I was living with my parents once again, feeling like I couldn't function and so distraught over what had happened to me (only later would I learn that this was all happening *for* me, as everything in my life had always been). I felt so angry at my boyfriend while simultaneously missing him, which felt extremely confusing to me. This was my first adult relationship, after all. The shame of leaving what I had thought was supposed to be my life felt unbearable. Everything I thought I knew about my future was crashing down before me, and I had absolutely no idea what I was going to do with my life. Then, I decided to go to Thailand for a few weeks on a backpacking trip with a friend who was in a similar position.

I had traveled a lot in my life, but I was spoiled when it came to vacation, used to luxury trips to the islands. Sure, I had stayed in hostels in Europe, but that was when I was a drunk college student trying to get by, but this was the first trip where I willingly put myself in a position of really "roughing it." I did things I never would have allowed myself to do before, like sleeping in the jungle and camping out on the beach. This trip opened my eyes to my ability to adapt to different environments. There was a lot of crying (and screaming about nearby animals), but I saw my resilience brought back to light. It was the adventure of a lifetime.

But then I came home, and for the next few months, I was right back in the same cycle, hating him while simultaneously missing him. I wasn't yet aware of my patterns or conscious of the fact that after childhood abuse, we are more likely to allow other people to treat us like shit. There were so many red flags I overlooked. By June, we were back together, and just like that, my life was back on track. Or so I thought. I had a great summer that year. I turned twenty-five. I was teaching some group classes at the gym where I previously worked because I enjoyed it and ended up getting a job as a marketing manager for a drink company. I was beyond excited, having always known I wanted to work for a brand because of how much I loved my internship with a coconut water company in college. It was the perfect job for me. I was on the road almost every day, could work from home, and got to coordinate events. Life was looking good. Then, something happened that once again put a wrench in my plans.

Part of my job was maintaining a storage unit filled with products and brand gear. On one occasion, I was asked to move a thousand twelve-bottle cases from one unit to another. Of course, I did it without a second thought. The next day, I woke up in terrible pain, unable to move my head. I went to the doctor and was told I couldn't work until I got better.

This began one of the most stressful times of my entire life. The girl who had had a job since she was nine years old and loved to keep herself busy, incapable of sitting still, was now on workers' comp, not permitted to do anything or else she would get in trouble. Looking back, I should have known this was a recipe for disaster.

I spent all my time trying to get better and thinking of ways to make money that didn't break the rules of workers' compensation. I wasn't able to teach classes at the gym because I was "injured" and was living rent-free at my parents' house, but the thought of not having a second income was enough to drive me absolutely insane. The anxiety constantly rushing through my body was something I would come to understand only later in life.

Over those months, I became an absolutely frantic mess of a human. I was extremely anxious, depressed, and in excruciating pain—more pain than made sense for the injury that had occurred. I had weekly massages, acupuncture, and physical therapy a few times a week but found little to no relief. I also started having horrible migraines and nausea, which we chalked up to post-concussion syndrome. I was told that the left side of my brain was seventeen percent weaker than my right and added vestibular therapy to the mix as a way to even out my brain.

Eventually, I went to the neurologist and demanded a full scan, only to be told that everything looked fine and that it seemed like I was just depressed. I'll never forget leaving that neurologist appointment, screaming and yelling about how stupid these people were. *Depressed?! I'm not fucking depressed! I know what depression feels like, and this is not it! What the actual fuck?* It was starting to feel like nothing would go my way.

During this time, I was spending a lot of time at my boyfriend's parents' house, where he was living in their basement. It was an hour drive from my parents in Waltham, but since I wasn't working, making the trip was no big deal. Plus, I absolutely loved his family. But then I would get there and have these little freak-out episodes, arriving and frantically organizing all the stuff in my bag, over and over. I wouldn't be able to sleep and was terrified to go to the bathroom in the middle of the night. Sometimes I would pee on a towel in the laundry room just so I wouldn't have to go upstairs. My fear was entirely irrational, similar to that of a young child who is afraid of the dark and the boogeyman.

I remember having several explosive episodes and not being able to sleep a wink. Everything seemed to add yet more stress to my already stressed body. I chalked it up to the pain. This dark place in my mind made me miserable, but it was not unfamiliar. My boyfriend, on the other hand, thought something was up—so much so that he gave me a book he thought might help.

How did I end up in this situation? Why did I hate myself so much? Why couldn't I be grateful for everything that I did have? From the outside, everything looked great, but on the inside, I was dying a little more every single day. Nothing about me made sense to me—or to anyone around me, for that matter.

That is until January 3, 2017, at 9:55 a.m., when one line in a book clicked everything off. All of the outlets I had previously used to dissociate from my memories were no longer an option. My mind and body finally had enough space to allow me to acknowledge the past. From that moment on, everything started to make perfect sense. Of course I hated myself and my body. Who wouldn't after being sexually abused? Maybe I wasn't some insane, ungrateful shell of a human. And so began the self-discovery journey I never asked for.

THE WHIPLASH OF REMEMBERING

The week the memory came back, I sat in the chair across from my therapist as I always did and told her about my revelations. I was scared shitless and didn't know how anyone was going to take this news. I questioned myself, thinking I must have made it up or seen it in a movie. But then I'd remember all the pain I'd felt for months and how it had vanished as soon as the memories arose. My body wasn't lying; it was my proof.

To my surprise, my therapist's reaction was almost identical to my own. She believed me and stated that now everything about me made perfect sense. With this single little memory (though really it wasn't little at all), we were both brought more clarity about me and my saga of drama than we had received from ten years of talking about my feelings and life events. I knew I wasn't bipolar; I was *traumatized*. How beautifully disappointing.

Once I remembered and my pain subsided, I was cleared

to go back to work. Perfect, I thought, welcoming the distraction from that mental image that would not stop popping up. Newsflash: This was not perfect at all. Little did I know that that memory would be the first of several to arise and explain my life in a way I could never have imagined. More and more flashbacks started coming to mind, like Polaroid images, of the many times my uncle inappropriately touched me. With the newfound information came new body sensations and intense emotional reactions I had no idea how to cope with. The past would hit me at random—sudden flashes of memory, physical sensations, smells, and tastes I couldn't escape. It was disturbing, unpredictable, and completely overwhelming.

My therapist, knowing she was not equipped to deal with this type of trauma, suggested I search for a trauma therapist. In the meantime, I had other problems to tackle, like how the fuck was I going to tell my family this news? There were so many questions floating around in my mind, driving me absolutely insane. Would they even believe me? How could I trust these memories? What if I *was* going absolutely insane?

On January 19, sixteen days after the first memory, I had my first trauma doctor appointment. I went in, seething with rage, wanting revenge for what had happened to me and ready to be better, to read whatever book they told me to and do any exercises they suggested. I sat down with the doctor, and she wrote something down on a piece of paper I still have to this day: "I am just coming to terms with what happened to me. I know I have the capacity to get better. People heal from trauma. My job is to go slow and work on my healing. I will heal and recover."

While this was a beautiful note, it did not sit well with my twenty-five-year-old self, who wanted to be better *right now*. Reading those words sparked a raging fire in me to declare then and there that I would do everything and anything to get better. Perhaps that wasn't the reaction my therapist had intended, but things have a way of working out the way they're meant to. No one was going to ruin my life. I was going to decide how this story ended. It was my declaration to God—and he sure must have received it.

After that initial trauma therapy session, things started to get very challenging on a personal level. My nervous system was soon overwhelmed by how many traumatic memories from my childhood and beyond I was recovering. The Universe was beginning to deliver the action steps for me to take, and it came at a price. Nevertheless, I persisted.

I made a plan with my long-term therapist to tell my parents within the next couple of weeks over a group session, deciding that would be the best way to handle the tough discussion. Apparently, though, my higher self had other plans. One night while sending an email at home, I was suddenly overcome by a hysterical crying fit. My dad heard me from another room in the small house and came over, trying to calm me down and assuring me that, whatever it was, it wasn't a big deal.

"It's only work," he told me.

I screamed back that he didn't understand, but he continued.

"Of course I do!" he said. "I've been working longer than you've been alive!"

It was then that I needed him to understand that this had nothing to do with work. I took one look at him and said,

"Uncle Malcolm abused me as a kid—that's why I'm crying. I've been having all of these flashbacks lately."

With a gasp, he pulled me into his arms without another word.

"How do we tell Mommy?" I continued, sobbing. "She won't believe her brother did such a thing. I don't want to ruin her life."

My dad assured me it would be okay, and that, together, we'd figure out a way to tell her. That she, too, would believe me.

In that moment, something else clicked for me. I had worried my dad didn't understand me and wouldn't be able to see me clearly, but maybe I had been the one not seeing myself. Maybe, because of that, I couldn't see others clearly either. When I saw that everything made sense to him, too, the perception I had of my life shifted yet again.

Later that night, we sat my mom down and explained what was going on. For her, too, it was like everything about me made sense now. My younger brother and sister gave the same reaction. There were lots of feelings from everyone, of course, but it's not my place to speak about anyone else's experience. I can only speak for myself, and I was beyond surprised that my family showed up for me in this way, believing what I told them even as I had feared they wouldn't. That day catapulted my entire family onto the journey of healing, and I was their leader.

We still went to that therapy session together, just like I'd planned with my therapist. Now, with everything out in the open, my family started actively looking for ways to support me. I bought a copy of *Trauma and Recovery* by Judith Herman and gave it to anyone who wanted to understand what I was going through—family, friends, whoever was willing to learn. It was my way of saying, "If you want to help me, start by understanding what this actually is."

After one particular conversation with my dad's side of the family, I went to my room, lay down on my bed, and suddenly felt like someone was physically touching me. Naturally, it freaked me out. My cousin, who was working on the psychiatric floor at the hospital, later told me that the reaction was totally normal—I was probably having a body flashback. I remember thinking, *Great, so now I've unlocked a new level of weird. Go me.*

That body flashback was the first of many that I would experience along my journey. It made me want to crawl out of my skin and was often accompanied by suicidal thoughts. Graphic visions of jumping off bridges, stabbing myself with knives, and driving my car off the side of the highway became my new normal. I could tolerate the thoughts because I always knew I wouldn't act on them, but that didn't make the experience any less exhausting. Looking back, I realize I'd been living with this kind of mental noise since I was a kid. Back then, I just pushed it all down, pretending it wasn't there or trying to distract myself. The only difference now was that I had language for what was happening. My body and mind were finally catching up to each other.

I started therapy in 2006 but refused to take medication or see a psychiatrist until 2012, when things got so bad I felt like I didn't have a choice. From then on, I stuck with the same psychiatrist and ran the full medication gauntlet: mood stabilizers like Lamictal and every sedative for anxiety—lorazepam, Xanax, Klonopin. I was prescribed an antipsychotic, which I tried for a few days, but it made me feel like I had holes in my brain. I tried trazadone for a bit and hated it, so I stopped that. Another time, gabapentin was added to the mix. I didn't have any reaction to that, so I kept it up. None of these were actually helping with my PTSD symptoms, yet, desperate for a cure, I continued to try the pills.

The cycle continued. The only thing I wouldn't touch were SSRIs. Every time they tried to get me on those, I'd look up the side effects, see "weight gain," and flush the pills down the toilet. As messed up as it sounds, gaining weight scared me more than staying unwell. That's how deep the shame and obsession went. By the time I finally agreed to meds, I was desperate for relief—but not if it meant sacrificing my body.

Then came my brilliant idea. I noticed that I seemed unable to concentrate at all and decided I had developed adult ADHD. I'd never had issues with the controlled substances I'd been prescribed before; if anything, I was careful, only taking them for sleep and even hoarding extras in case I ran out. But Adderall? This drug was different; I was actually excited about it. I thought it would finally give me energy, help me focus, and—bonus—suppress my appetite so I could get skinnier. Hell yeah. It felt like the jackpot.

My psychiatrist didn't hesitate to write the script, even though she told me with every single visit that no medication could actually solve what I was dealing with. I remember thinking, *What the actual fuck am I doing? Why am I swallowing pills when even my doctor admits they won't help?* But I ignored those thoughts and kept taking whatever she gave me, always somehow hoping that something would finally work.

The medication often confused me and blocked my emotions, and in retrospect, I would have preferred to connect with my body and feel my feelings, as overwhelming as they were. But once I was on the pills, I was advised to keep taking them for my own safety. I listened, believing that doctors knew my body better than I did. After all, I didn't understand how I was feeling or what was happening to me. None of that was ever explained to me; I was just given a pill and told, "See you next time!" Sometimes we need medication—and that's okay—but by no means is it the cure to our emotional issues. It would take me years to break this pattern of always doing what I was told rather than listening to my body, trusting others rather than myself.

So there I was, twenty-five years old, having just realized the abuse I suffered as a child, and taking daily doses of Lamictal, Adderall, gabapentin, and a regular rotation of Xanax, Klonopin, and lorazepam. To paint the picture, as soon as I woke up, I'd pop my mood stabilizer and an Adderall (AKA, "let's numb our feelings and shoot our energy through the roof"). I was all drugged up and ready to do the work—until midday, when the Adderall would wear off and I'd have to take my prescription meth for another jolt of energy. Then I'd finish the day off by drugging myself unconscious with the sedatives. All of this, and yet my main concern was whether Adderall would help me get skinny.

As I embarked on my healing journey, I noticed I had spent years harboring resentment toward others and now realized it had nothing to do with them and everything to do with what I experienced as a child. It suddenly felt really important to me that the people in my life understood and heard directly from my mouth that I was not actually a miserable and ungrateful human with crippling anxiety. I felt an overwhelming need to express my truth and explain that my innocence had been stolen from me and that I was so sorry for projecting my pain onto them.

Starting with my relatives, I apologized for having felt like they didn't love me, for leaving family events, and for harboring resentment in the past. They were all extremely receptive and agreed that everything about me made perfect sense. Now they all understood why my Uncle Malcolm "disappeared" when I was five years old for over twelve years and why he was divorced by his wife for "some reason." My apologies were well received, and my family has offered their full support to this day.

Next, I shared my recent self-awareness with my friends, co-workers, and clients. Over and over again, I was shown the same supportive reactions. In fact, to my surprise, the more people I told, the more I learned how many others had had similar experiences. I realized my burning desire to tell my truth was not only for me but also to shed light on a subject that feels shameful to so many of us.

Then, it was time to go to my Uncle Jeremy's house to tell him and his family what happened and see if he or Auntie Donna remembered anything about the incidents involving his brother. I felt so relieved and validated as my mother, father, sister, and brother accompanied me for the gathering. We drove the forty-five minutes and sat down with our relatives. I was nervous but felt safe and protected by my dad, strong, bold, and confident yet gentle as he proceeded to tell his brother-in-law that I had PTSD and that it was because Uncle Malcolm had sexually abused me as a kid.

My aunt gasped and grabbed my arm as soon as my father uttered the words.

"Well, what did he do to you?" Uncle Jeremy asked after taking a deep breath, looking me dead in the eye.

"No, please don't tell us!" my cousins screamed and yelled in the background, not wanting to hear the awful truth.

"Tell us what you remember," my uncle continued.

Having received so much support from others thus far, the response floored me. The last thing I wanted was to detail my disturbing memories aloud. I had relived them enough as it was.

Finally, I answered him and watched him sit back in shock. My mom took the chance to chime in, asking questions about why Malcolm and his wife got a divorce. They couldn't remember—something had happened with their daughter.

"It was nothing," Uncle Jeremy said, perking up. "He was just jerking off in bed next to her."

I was livid, thinking about what abuse may have taken place in their home, but my mom interrupted my outburst with another question.

"Do you remember the time Gabriella had her period on the slide at your house?"

My aunt claimed she had no memory of that (interesting that someone with only sons wouldn't remember the time her niece bled profusely while under her supervision). Soon after, we said our goodbyes and made our way back home.

Ultimately, my relatives said they believed me, but the fact that they couldn't remember what had happened and the way they questioned me after I shared something so vulnerable were very different from my other experiences of sharing my story. Still, I was so focused on fighting for my internal sense of safety. I might've noticed the red flags, but I couldn't process them yet.

Regardless of that unpleasant interaction, I found immense relief in speaking my truth to the people in my life. Expressing my experience not only allowed me to feel supported by my family and friends, but it also set me on a new stage of healing. I established safety by expressing myself and allowing my truth to be heard, seen, and supported. This was crucial for me. However, it also caused more memories to come to the surface, leaving me to learn how to cope by myself.

You see, I didn't end up going back to that initial trauma doctor. She told me she didn't feel she was fit to help me, something I would grow accustomed to hearing. So I was on the hunt once again for the right doctor, but I kept encountering the same issue: these doctors who didn't know me would tell me that since my memories had been repressed for so long, they might not be real and couldn't be trusted. I learned that some doctors don't believe in repressed memories at all. I was even told that I had "false memories," which really sent me into a spiral. This felt confusing and detrimental to me, who had such a deep belief that doctors had it all figured out—they knew it all, and I was their patient waiting to be saved by their greater-than-thou knowledge.

Their concerns reminded me of my initial doubts about whether I could trust what my mind was showing me, but my mind was persistent. My entire life, I had had dreams around this theme of abuse. In one specific dream, I was standing in the middle of a group of boys who were all jerking off around me. I was so disturbed by the dream that I told my therapist. Later, I came to recall that exact scenario as a childhood memory. My dreams had been telling me the truth of what had happened to me all along, but the doctors seemed to view me as crazy.

My therapist, whom I had been seeing for ten years, was certain I hadn't made any of it up. The memories were so graphically detailed, and I fully experienced them in the present moment. "How would you have made that up?" she would ask me. "What would make you come up with something like that?" I agreed with her—how *could* I make up something so vile? Me, who didn't even watch horror movies. Now it made sense why, when I started seeing Dr. Young at fifteen, she told me she had never heard of anyone with dreams as graphic as mine. She also suggested I write a book someday. (Thank you, Dr. Young.)

When the memories started, my dreams, too, mirrored the intensity of the flashbacks. After years of dissociating from the pain, now I couldn't escape it. I saw it unwillingly while I was awake and was fully immersed in it while asleep. Yet, for months, I continued to question my new reality. How could this have happened to me? Could it really be true? One second, I would stand in my truth and receive the external validation, then, I would be consumed by self-doubt, preferring to ruminate rather than face the pain. I didn't understand the concept of boundaries within my internal world, and everything felt overwhelmingly confusing. My mind still didn't want to accept what I had experienced, but I knew my body wasn't lying.

The way my physical self was expressing itself to me was unlike anything I had experienced before. I would feel sudden sharp pains in my vagina or hands on my chest or detect smells that weren't there. It made me feel absolutely insane, but I knew I wasn't because my memories correlated with the sensations I was experiencing. My body was speaking to me even when my mind struggled to make sense of it all.

If you are reading this and having a similar experience, I want you to know that you can trust yourself. Others might not understand, but that doesn't mean it isn't real or true. If it is real and true to *you*, that is enough. Reassuring yourself that it is real can help relieve some of the pain that may come up. The more we resist it, the more pain tries to penetrate its way through. Offering yourself trust and compassion is the way through this portion of the journey.

Meanwhile, I was having flashbacks—all day, every day—and searching for something to help me. On top of these doctors continually telling me they couldn't tell me if my memories were real, I was also being told that I was not to contact my abuser or go to the police to report the abuse because I was in a fragile state and it may harm me. This pissed me off. There was nothing I wanted more than to scream at my Uncle Malcolm and tell him what a piece of shit he was for doing this to me. I wanted to drive down to the Randolph police and tell them everything in detail so that this motherfucker could go to jail, where he belonged. My worst fear was that I wasn't the only one and there would be even more in the future. Abusers don't just abuse one kid. It's an illness, a manifestation of a demon, that takes over a person's soul and causes them to harm children.

I knew I needed more therapy—something trauma-related, but I wasn't sure what. I was open to it all. But I listened to the doctors because I believed they must know better than me. What I didn't realize at that time was that I didn't have to search for help; the help was going to find me.

Looking back now, I understand that telling me not to pursue immediate action was good advice. At the initial remembrance of any trauma, it feels heavy and unbearable. Without proper processing or grounding tools, it can be harmful to the psyche and may put you back in a position of feeling invalidated.

The process to lessen these feelings starts with accepting where you are. Healing takes time, and though we are not alone in it, it's important to have a toolbox of skills we can rely on to recenter ourselves before entering a perceived space of danger.

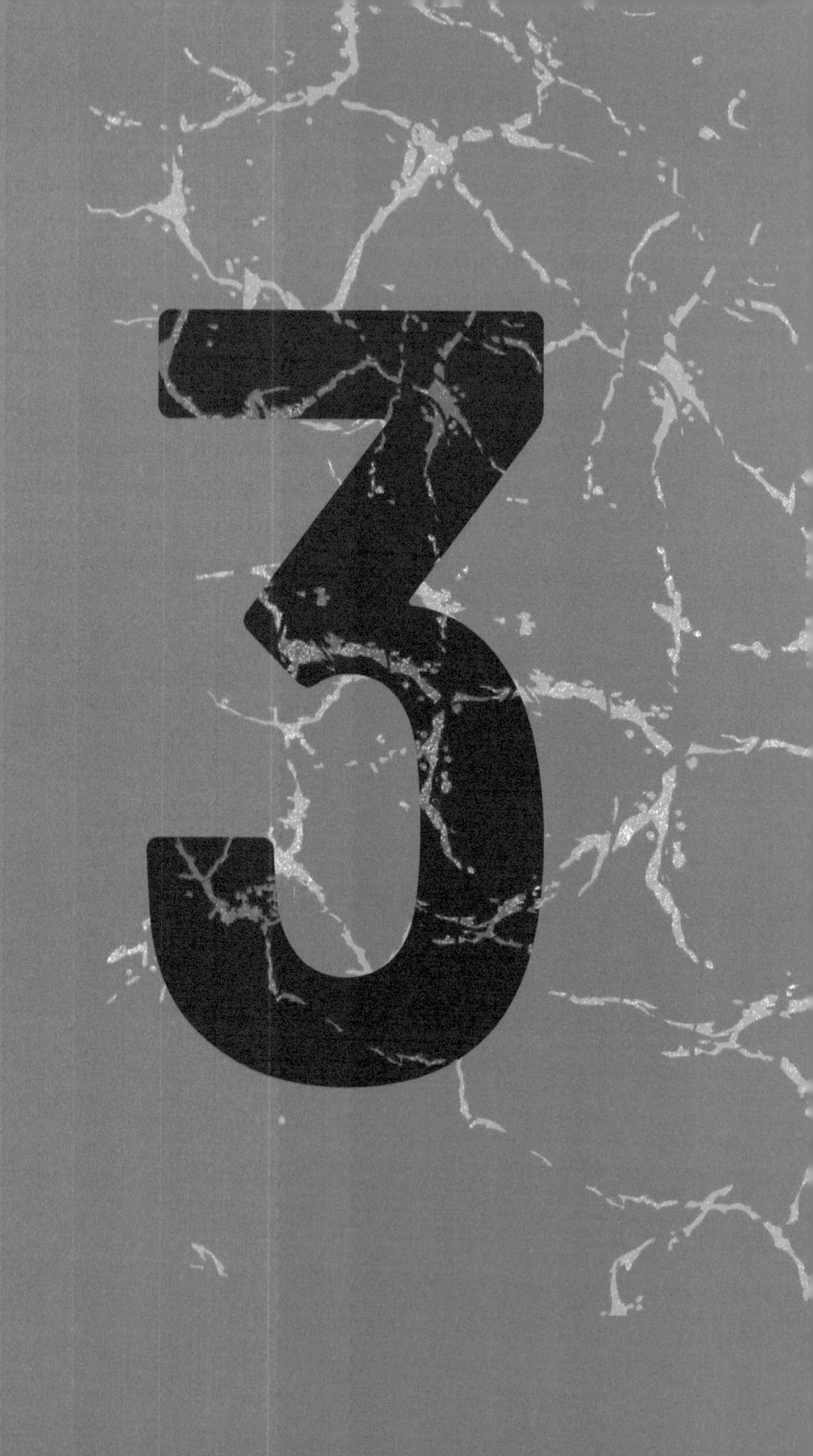

WHEN LIFE HANDS YOU HELL, BUILD A TOOLBOX

One of the most interesting things about my journey was that the more I expressed my authentic self—no matter how fucked up or messy she was—the more I saw the puzzle pieces fall into place. It defied logic, literally magically. The more I learned to lean on God (or Source or the Universe or whatever you want to call a Higher Power) and not my own will, the easier my journey got.

One way I leaned into my true self and allowed myself to live authentically was by following my inner guidance to tell more friends about what had happened to me, even as I sometimes judged myself for doing so. I didn't quite understand why I felt the need to share this hard truth, but I always did it anyway. I could no longer lie or pretend that I was okay. I *wasn't* okay, and I wanted to express that.

I was catching up over the phone with an out-of-state friend one day. When I shared what had happened to me, I was immediately told that it had happened to her too. We talked for hours, and she told me I should read *The Power of Positive Thinking*. She told me it was all about gratitude, seeing the positive in everything, and shifting your reality. Soon after, I started reading the book, and my entire worldview changed (I even got a wrist tattoo taken from it). I immediately put its wisdom into practice. I started a gratitude journal, began writing Bible verses down daily, and even though I was still experiencing internal hell, found time to notice positive things about each and every day.

I hadn't been the most positive person, so this was very different for me. I wasn't usually the type to see the best in things and was always searching for what could go wrong—and I didn't see anything wrong with that way of living. Honestly, I didn't think much about it. But once I shifted to a more intentional way of thinking and feeling, I saw profound benefits. It was the beginning of my journey to realizing my energy was what created my reality. Even on my "bad days," I was still able to somehow shift my energy. Like so many of the resources I discovered at this point, I wish I had found this book earlier. The funny thing about trauma is how it sometimes serves us in ways we wouldn't expect. But everything happens for us exactly when it's meant to. I started to see that amid life's ups and downs, moments of intense joy and horrible pain, we're always being guided exactly where we are meant to be.

Not long after, I was introduced to Rosanne, an amazing older woman who was also a sexual-abuse survivor. My father's sister, Aunt MaryJo, had introduced us in the hopes that Rosanne might provide some guidance for my own healing. At the time, Rosanne was battling in a court case with her abuser, and she also told me about a Dialectical Behavior

Therapy (DBT) outpatient program for women with PTSD at McLean Hospital. She had done the program multiple times and thought I would benefit from it too.

Meeting Rosanne, I felt so seen and understood. I was enthusiastic to do anything to get better, and a two-week outpatient program didn't sound so bad. I applied for the program right away, but there was a two-year waitlist. *Oh well,* I remember thinking, *I'll just keep searching for something else.*

Until that point, I had felt so lonely, even as I was surrounded by loved ones who wanted to help and just didn't understand how to do so. Rosanne gave me tangible hope that there were resources out there for me and that I could get better and find justice. She also gave me a red bracelet that another survivor had given her, a symbol of the journey we were both on. I wore that thing every single day for three years until I would eventually pass it along to another younger survivor. Sometimes, we don't realize the weight our stories carry and how they can help others in profound ways.

Then, to my surprise, no fewer than two weeks later, I got a call from the outpatient program saying there was an open spot for me. I guess my positive thinking really was working. I was nervous but excited to start working on my healing and learn the things that were necessary to handle PTSD. I was thrilled to finally have an avenue to "be healed," but I also knew I wouldn't have full control over myself. At any moment, I could be triggered into another world of pain. What if this therapy sent me there? What if I wasn't able to come back?

The time flew by until I was on my way to the DBT program. During my initial intake, I encountered the same medical opinions I had grown used to hearing: The PTSD is real, but the memories might not be. What I think they meant is that even if our memories might not be one hundred percent accurate, the trauma we have experienced is real. But it sounded so silly to me. Everyone agreed that I had PTSD. How would I have just developed it out of thin air?

I arrived early on the first day of the program, looking extra cute with my Lululemon outfit and sparkly bag. I smiled at the other women and noticed I wasn't met with the same respect, but I brushed it off, thinking maybe they were just in their own worlds, nervous like me. For the next two weeks, the DBT therapy became the starter kit in the toolbox of coping skills, strategies, and mindset shifts that I would build over time. We learned about mindfulness, interpersonal effectiveness, emotional regulation, distress tolerance, and PTSD coping strategies, and with each new concept introduced, I was able to see the world completely differently, even if the actual integration of these practices would take time.

Prior to learning about mindfulness, I had no concept of simply being present in the moment. I had always either occupied some past or future headspace. This new principle would be the motivator for my future meditation practice. Interpersonal effectiveness showed me how and where in my relationships I was not showing up as I would like to. I had never been good at vocalizing my needs, so when they weren't met, I often lashed out or went silent instead of taking responsibility for how I was expressing myself. I began to learn how to effectively communicate with others and express my needs, something I hadn't even realized I didn't know how to do.

Emotional regulation was another shock to my system. I began to learn about my emotions, how to identify them, what they were actually telling me, and where they showed up in my body. That aching feeling in my heart? Fear. The nausea in my stomach? Shame. It was like opening up a whole new world of my lived experience.

Then there was distress tolerance—how to manage emotions without feeling overwhelmed and either exploding or indulging in self-harming behaviors. For a very long period of time, I restricted my food intake, over-exercised, and self-isolated when I was feeling overwhelmed. I could finally see these patterns and slowly begin unlearning them.

Finally, I learned the art of identifying activities and practices to bring myself back to the present moment. I learned about suppressed trauma and that when we are overwhelmed by traumatic experiences at a young age, we protect ourselves from the painful experiences by completely leaving our bodies, known as dissociation. Unfortunately, though, the pain does not disappear; it gets stored in the body only to be experienced at a later date. I had begun to allow this pain to move through me when I expressed my truth to my family. Doing so helped me feel safe and catalyzed my body to begin processing my experiences. I now understood that healing wasn't about escaping my pain, but learning how to ground myself through small, mindful actions. It's not always pretty, but it's real and it works.

The program was so helpful, but still, I left every day feeling as angry as ever. One o'clock would roll around, and I'd find myself pissed off and irritable. I chalked it up to the way the instructors spoke to me and how it made me feel belittled. It wasn't until one day in meditation that I had a full-circle memory and it all made sense. As I sat in meditation, I saw the clock strike one o'clock and remembered being four years old and my uncle taking my food away until I let him abuse me. I realized my anger didn't actually have anything to do with the teachers and had everything to do with my wounded inner child who was still triggered by the clock striking one o'clock, feeling hungry and rebelling against anyone she felt was "in charge" of her. Oh, how beautifully complex our brains and bodies are. I still had a long way to go when it came to coping with my PTSD, but I was grateful for the tools that enabled me to start making these connections over time.

Each day, I'd show up to McLean surrounded by the same negative attitudes I had been met with on day one. But I chose to continue leading with my newfound perspective of positivity, recognizing that not everybody wants to heal or look on the bright side. Some people are addicted to their own pain and suffering and aren't willing to let go of their perceptions, even if doing so would bring them freedom. When we experience heavy trauma, we often "marry" our story, living it out over and over again. The pain, although it may not be fun to experience, is comfortable, and letting go of these narratives comes with the discomfort of change, which many people aren't willing to or don't know how to move through. I, however, was not going to be one of those people. Even in the darkest hours, I would force myself to move forward.

This doesn't make me special or superior to any of the other program participants, but it does show that even if we come from similar circumstances and learn the same material, what we consistently choose to believe has an impact on our trajectory. I chose to believe that this therapy would push me forward. We were women of all ages, backgrounds, education levels, families, and so on, and yet we all struggled with the same issue. It was up to each of us to hold an opinion on how this treatment would impact us. Would we take these lessons and implement them, knowing they could help us? Or would we choose to make excuses for our lives and blame our past for the way we showed up in the world?

Was this DBT therapy the thing that healed me? Absolutely not. Did it push me to expand my thoughts and perception of myself, the world, and how I was showing up in it? Absolutely. So often, we search for a cure for something, not realizing that the cure lies right within us. The way we think and feel has more power than we sometimes like to admit. We get to decide how we feel, and then that becomes our truth.

I often left the program wondering why they never taught us any of this at school, a question that legitimately still puzzles me. I would imagine what my life could have looked like had I had these tools when I was younger. Even just the skills to properly communicate how I was feeling and knowing how to ask for what I wanted could have been life-changing. Now that I had these tools, I felt so deeply that this needed to be taught to everyone, yet I knew that going back to school wasn't in the cards for me. I was already drowning in student loans from undergrad, and if I took the time to go back, I would be stuck at my parents' house until I was forty.

I had learned from one of the program therapists that there were three phases of trauma healing: safety and stabilization (the stage I was in during the program); processing and integration; and, finally, connecting with others. I trusted that I would somehow find a way to teach these things, but my first priority had to be about creating the safety I needed within myself.

Each of us at the DBT program was assigned a social worker. I had the opportunity to meet with two different women, whom I liked a lot. They were a lot like me and seemed like people I would hang out with. At the time, I was boxing almost every day, and they suggested I stop any exercise that evoked anger while I was in the program. Apparently, when you're already in a state of perpetual anger, fueling it further isn't so great for the nervous system. The women advised that I, instead, try activities that may be calming to my nervous system and establish safety in the body. They hadn't given any specific suggestions, but I found a yoga studio a couple of towns over and decided to give it a try.

When I walked into my first class there, I was shocked to see that one of the social workers was also the yoga instructor and that the other social worker was also in attendance. There are plenty of yoga studios in my hometown, but now I knew why something had compelled me to choose this one. Due to the rule that discourages public acknowledgement between client and therapist for privacy reasons, the three of us did nothing more than exchange knowing glances. But once I ran into them at yoga after completing the DBT program, we would speak with each other and keep up our connection, just as I had thought we would. The rest is history.

It was what I would come to refer to as God winks, the Universe's way of providing coincidences in my outer world that were really not coincidences at all, moments in time where everything just made sense. These were like divine intervention, signs from heaven that I was doing the right thing.

The yoga studio ended up holding more significance than I could ever have expected. Each class spoke deeper to my soul, providing an emotional release on the mat and connecting me to my truth as I flowed. As someone who had used exercise as a way to punish myself in the past, always in pursuit of altering how I looked, yoga taught me to appreciate my body and feel all my feelings. I slowly began to feel at home in my own skin.

I was still experiencing the past in my body, but yoga made it easier to cope, giving me a way back into my body when everything within me wanted to escape it. It helped me feel safe enough to notice the sensations without spiraling into the story. Over time, I started to realize that my intense emotions were just energy—moving, shifting, releasing. Yoga became a space where I could process without words, where my body could speak and I could finally listen.

The yoga studio is also where I was introduced to weed as a healing medicine. Mary, another instructor I felt very connected to, gave speeches before and after class that always seemed to resonate with me. One day, we got to talking after class about my experience with PTSD. She understood and comforted me, letting me know that she had had a similar experience and found weed really helpful. The next time I went to her class, she had brought a pipe and some weed for me.

I had only tried weed once or twice before and tended to stay away from mind-altering substances, but I trusted Mary's insights and gave it a try. This time, it didn't take me out of my experience and actually helped me see things more clearly, moving out my old energy and making me feel lighter and happier. Plant medicine may not work for everyone, but it was a very helpful tool for me on top of all the pills I was still taking.

At the beginning of my journey, the bulk of my energy was continually spent going outside of myself. I had a deep desire to expose my abusers, seek justice, and find a professional to "tell me what to do" so I could get better. It wasn't until after my two weeks at the DBT program that I began to realize that it was an internal game I was playing, and the only person I was playing against was myself.

One day, while I was lying in bed scrolling on my iPad, I found a book called *Why Can't I Meditate?* by Nigel Wellings. Curious about the idea of meditation after my lessons on mindfulness, I started reading and learned that people struggle to meditate when they are afraid to see their true selves. We bury ourselves beneath anxiety and tasks, and it is challenging to actually sit down and connect to who we really are. I realized meditation was a gradual practice, not something I could jump into full-force.

I found a series called *Fuck That* meditations online—gritty, witty, and only a minute long. I loved the clarity I felt after even a minute of doing them and, after a couple of days, decided to expand my horizons with other YouTube creators. Within a month, I was deep diving into my subconscious mind for fifteen minutes or more, guided by Jason Stephenson, Michael Sealy, and Joe Treacy.

I started to turn to meditation whenever I felt over-whelmed. It became my saving grace after nights when I got too little sleep. I would carve out time for meditation and receive the energy I needed to make it through the day.

Meditating had finally made me feel connected to my true self, calm and at peace. The noise of the outside world would quietly disappear, and I was finally able to witness myself as I was. The practice became everything to me.

As the days passed, my meditations got deeper and longer, until I started practicing hour-and-a-half-long sessions. I found myself oddly attracted to what I then thought was "random" hypnoses, often entitled things like "Meet your twin flame," "Meet your spirit guides," and "Access the Akashic records." I had no idea what any of these things meant, but they allowed my mind and body to relax.

Meditation was a tool that helped me, but it's important to keep in mind that I wasn't actively seeking answers in my meditations; they would just come to me over time. Looking back, the pattern is really clear: I would find safety in my body or outer world, and then a new memory would pop up for me to look at and process. I knew that what I fed my mind would manifest into my reality. I just didn't get to choose when, where, or how (wink, wink).

As my meditation deepened, so did my anger and resentment toward my Uncle Malcolm for what he did to me. Over time, I remembered more than I would have liked to, and it was hard for me to understand what to do with all of this new knowledge. If you are experiencing this or fear that you may in the future, I'd like to offer you a tool that I wish I had had in those moments: When memories come up, you can tell them, "Thank you, but not right now," and then wipe them away with your hands before tapping on your chest to bring yourself back to the present moment, allowing whatever emotion is coming up to move through your body.

Though they were still unpleasant to relive, I noticed that my memories were getting easier to cope with. I was actively implementing the skills and grounding techniques I had learned at the DBT program, and they continued to be extremely helpful. We had a running joke in my house that I would go to my "toolbox" to continually soothe myself and cope with whatever old and new traumas were coming through. I can't even count the hours I spent doing crafts, adult coloring books, word searches, anything to get out of my head and into the present moment. I often sat in the living room under a depression lamp, making card craft and bedazzling glasses and jars as a distress tolerance skill when I experienced overwhelming flashbacks.

Some say we experience several ego deaths in a lifetime. I've had my share, but nothing has shaken my world like when I remembered my childhood trauma. When pain like that surfaces, there is no knowing what to do with it. Others tried to help, and I was told "it will get better" more times than I can count, but when you're that low, words like that feel empty at best and insulting at worst.

What actually helped wasn't pity; it was finding ways to be real with myself. Slowly, I built my own toolbox—one that actually worked for me. Instead of hiding, I learned how to sit with my truth, let the feelings move, and honor the messiness of healing. Sometimes, that meant watching shows or movies with characters who'd gone through similar things just so I could feel less alone, giving myself permission to feel and see that I wasn't the only one carrying this kind of pain.

The process, as brutal as it was, is what ultimately taught me to trust myself again. Healing wasn't about erasing the pain or pretending I was okay. It was about showing up for myself, honestly and fully, over and over, until that trust felt real.

PARTS, PIECES, AND THE PUZZLE OF ME

Between meditation, yoga, and talk therapy, I started to find myself moving forward from where I had been a few months prior and coming to terms with the idea that what had happened to me was real. Every time I assured myself I was going to be okay and that things would get better, really embracing that attitude without a doubt, I was greeted with a new memory to process. *What?* I would think. *How are there more?* And here is the kicker: Each memory that came seemed worse than the one prior. It made me absolutely furious. I felt betrayed by my own brain and by God. How had he let this happen to me?

Prior to all the memories, prayer was part of my everyday practice, particularly before I went to sleep at night. I had always had trouble sleeping, and this ritual was my way of connecting with God. I was taught when I was a child to say the "Our Father" and "Hail Mary" and ask God to bless the people in my life by name.

Then, as the memories kept coming to me, I suddenly found myself unable to pray, literally unable to remember the words to the prayers I'd been saying my whole life. I remember lying in bed and trying to remember the words. I was so confused, feeling uneasy every time I had to look up the words on my phone. It was as if the prayers had been completely erased from my memory, like my mind was being robbed by the parts of me that had endured the abuse. The parts of me that had no hope or faith and just wanted to die.

During these times, I would scream and cry to my parents that I felt the devil was inside of me—the only label my mind could think to give the trauma that was stored in my body. I sensed a dark energy living within me, so strong that I could feel, hear, taste, and smell it. It felt so real to me because it *was* real. It became a custom in my house to throw water on me, make me sniff ammonia, or place a cold ice pack on my body to bring me back.

What surprised me was that when I really committed to healing, things didn't get easier right away. In fact, everything got louder. More memories surfaced. More pain. More confusion. For a while, it felt like I was getting worse instead of better. That's something no one really tells you—healing can be just as painful as the injury. The difference was that, this time, the pain was moving through me. It was no longer stuck. It wasn't proof that I was broken; it was proof that my system was finally safe enough to release what had been stored for so long.

Even through these times, I held dual beliefs about my experiences. I still had moments when I thought I must have made this up. It was too much, too cruel—who could do this to a child, let alone their own flesh and blood? But, again, whenever I would deny my reality, my body would revolt. Body flashbacks galore! It occurred in real time, so much so that at one point I woke up from my meditation with a full-on hand mark pressed on my beating red chest, my heart racing. I would experience waves of unbearable pain that would last for weeks, yet, somehow, I'd always find my way out of it.

It's important to understand that healing our emotions doesn't mean they'll never show up again. The healing is learning how to tolerate them rather than pushing them away. People often say that God only gives us what we can handle. Our minds work the same way. If you're not feeling safe right now, it's okay. Establishing a grounding practice or slowing down your waking life can help ease you into allowing the memories to come forward. As I have seen from my own experience and the experience of my clients, I truly believe this to be true.

The remembrance and release of trauma has no agenda or timeline; its only goal is to be seen, accepted, and integrated into our experience. The way my memories presented themselves did not honor any chronological timeline; they were just dropped in for me to figure out. It became a puzzle for me to piece together. I started to keep records of the visual memories, body memories, and emotional flashbacks and triggers as I experienced them. Everything in my life became this game of trying to figure myself out for my own sanity's sake.

The recollection of trauma brings along the lower energies and emotions that are living in the body waiting to be released. If they're not processed, these feelings can leave us feeling stuck in the past, unable to feel at peace. In fact, the more we repress them, the more they act like sneaky little ninjas, waiting to tear us down at any moment without forewarning. Repressing emotions is similar to taking out a loan; you may be buying time, but eventually you're going to have to pay up—perhaps with monthly fees or perhaps whenever the loan shark comes after you. The choice is up to you and your body.

While I was healing, I made the mistake of trying to ascribe meaning to the feelings I was experiencing. I wanted to feel like there was a reason behind each and every emotion, that they weren't just part of my old story and that everything had to come from somewhere or mean something about me. Sometimes, though, these emotions arise simply because they never had the chance to before, whether sparked by an obvious trigger or simply releasing because the body finally feels safe enough to let something go. Feelings don't always arrive with context or clarity, and they don't need a reason to be there. They just need space to move. Sometimes, feelings are just feelings.

Soon, I started to notice that it wasn't only the words to prayers I was forgetting. It was like the newfound memories from my past were making it more and more difficult to recall anything in my waking life, even simple conversations. I'll never forget when I was sitting at the kitchen counter with my boss boyfriend (we were still trying to make it work), and he said, "Okay, let's go!" I looked at him and said, "What are you talking about? Go where?" He stared at me, shocked, explaining that we had literally just been talking about going to the grocery store. I immediately burst into tears. I couldn't remember what was happening because I was not present. This was the first time I realized how much I was still dissociating.

It sent me spiraling, agonizing about how many other conversations had taken place that I wasn't remembering. I wondered who these parts of me were that fully functioned without my even noticing, a scary thought for that version of me who didn't yet know how to ground and stay present. For someone who was hyper-vigilant, the thought of not being in control of myself was heart-wrenching as well as extremely embarrassing. I felt like I had something new to worry about. Had this been my reality for twenty-five years, and I was just now realizing it? I would soon discover what was really going on inside my body.

I knew that what I was experiencing had to be deeper than just the abuse and what I was addressing in therapy. I was extremely curious about the "parts" of me that showed up during my meditations, and if no doctor was going to help me figure them out, I was going to take personal responsibility and do it myself. I knew these different parts were all me, but they all seemed to have their own identities, energies, thoughts, and feelings. Each of them had a story to tell, complete with visual evidence, physical feelings, visceral smells, and potent tastes that I experienced in my body.

One day, when I was getting rid of old stuff in my parents' basement, I found a notebook my aunt had given me when I was eleven for "daydreams and doodles." I sat down and flipped through the pages of what my pre-teen self had written. With every word I read, including song lyrics about wanting to die and feeling misunderstood, I could feel the pain of younger me. Then, I flipped to a page that yet again changed everything. There were two columns: "Nicknames I like" and "Nicknames I don't like." As I read through the twenty-five names that followed, I could feel the parts within me ignite.

Between the dissociating I was experiencing, the memories, and the parts in my meditations, I was blown away. Had I created multiple personalities that I had no recollection of? I had heard of people with dissociative identity disorder, and accepting this label helped my ego get on board with feeling it was something that could be healed. And people had wondered why I couldn't work full-time. Co-existing with all these new insights *was* a full-time job.

When I speak about this experience, it's just to show you where my mind was at and how I was coping with my experience. As an older version of me writing this to you, I want you to know that you don't require a label in order to heal. In the early stages of my healing, I didn't understand that there was nothing wrong with me; I had just been through horrific things. I thought it was my job to "fix" myself and change everything about me. But real healing is in accepting yourself exactly as you are and learning to love all parts of you. The creation of these other "parts" of me is what allowed me to survive, to live a "normal" life and function in society. One could even argue that they were the reason I did so well in my life, allowing me to adapt to environments and change myself in order to keep myself safe. After discovering the journal, I did some research and learned about IFS, or Internal Family Systems therapy, used to heal wounded parts of a patient's psyche in order to find balance and access their true self. I immediately bought a book and began applying the IFS techniques I learned. Here is an excerpt from an exercise I did on June 5, 2017:

True life: I have three personalities.

Gabriella, 4-8 years old: Depressed, guilty, shameful, dependent; doesn't leave the house unless her family is with her. Gabriella is a daughter and a sister. She fights and is angry at home. She hates the world and wishes she were gone and never had to come back. She doesn't want to live like this. No one wants to play with Gabriella.

Gabby, 5-25: People pleaser; submissive. Gabby is who I am when I am pretending to be okay. Gabby is what the world wants to see and not what she really is. She is a good actress and very charming. She has a pretty smile, and everyone wants to be around her. Everyone thinks Gabby is beautiful, smart, and fun. Everyone wants to play with Gabby.

Gab, now-future: Independent, smart, strong. Gab is the integration of a little bit of Gabriella and Gabby. People who know Gab can see the anxiety but also the happiness. The anxiety is kept under control and doesn't explode. Gab knows Gabriella and Gabby, but I don't think they know about her.

Gabriella gets yelled at and cries hysterically. Gabby doesn't fight or argue, doesn't like getting yelled at, and she is afraid of getting in trouble. Gabby listens to what she is told to do because that is the only way she gets positive attention. She gets praise for being a good girl. Gab gets in arguments and uses her words like a big girl.

When Gabriella is around her family, she gets snippy and angry, but then sometimes Gab will show up and say a joke. Gabriella's parents don't know Gab very well, but maybe someday they will.

Gabby always lets things go and lets people stomp all over her. She is a wimp. Everyone always talks to Gabriella about their problems, but no one ever listens to her. She always does things for others, but no one does anything for her. Gab needs to start taking more control over her future.

Gabriella thinks no one loves her and has no friends. Gabby hears that people love her but sometimes questions whether she has friends. Gab knows that she has family and friends who love her.

All three of us don't understand why this is happening.

After years of feeling "off" and experiencing sensations that were accompanied by narratives that didn't feel like mine or didn't correspond to situations I was in, I was beginning to uncover the parts of me that were running the show I called life. It started to make sense why, as a grown woman, words like "No one wants to play with me" would come out of my mouth when I was sad or bored. This new self-awareness also shed light on why people would comment to my parents about how I had been such a kind, sweet child, to which they would reply, "Are we talking about the same kid?" At home, I was fiery, loud, and talked back a lot, often sent to my room for my "big mouth" and always needing to have the last word. All along, parts of me were being activated without my conscious knowledge; my inner turmoil made perfect sense.

I discovered several guided PTSD visualizations for trauma relief. Yet again, I fell in love with how I was able to escape the reality of my mind and doze off into a beautiful world surrounded by the ocean and flowers. I established this safe place for myself, and the work began to happen. I got to a place where I would do an hour or more of self-hypnosis. That's when the full memories of my past trauma began to resurface. I would be in meditation, minding my own business and feeling fantastic, only to be bombarded by full-on movies of the abuse in crystal clear images. Still, I didn't want to believe it, thinking that maybe I just had a wild imagination, distrusting myself just like the doctors had.

I would ask myself to show me what I looked like, how old I was and what my hair was like, gathering information and allowing myself to see the scenes play out. When the meditations finished and I would come back to the present, I'd go searching throughout the house for clues about what I saw. My parents kept a million photos of us in boxes, and, without fail, I always found confirmation of exactly what my mind had told me, down to the date. *Holy fucking shit*, I thought. My subconscious had been storing these memories all along, and parts of me had protected me by keeping them covered up.

Reconciling memories and body memories is one of the most disorienting parts of trauma healing, like trying to put together a thousand-piece puzzle with half of the pieces still hidden under the couch. I felt like my body and my mind were in completely different lifetimes, my mind saying, "You're probably making this up," while my body screamed, "Gabriella, we've been through hell!"

As I dug deeper, I was introduced to even more fragmented parts of my fragmented self, specifically those I had created to hold the trauma and pain I experienced. Going back to the list of names I created as a child, "Gabbith" popped out to me. I recognized most of the nicknames, but this one puzzled me. Who the fuck was Gabbith? No one ever called me that.

Not long after, Gabbith decided to present herself to me. She first showed up as a seven-year-old in a witch costume. During meditation, she showed me full visuals of a sleepover at a friend's house. We were watching *Arachnophobia*, and I was scared shitless. She also showed me bobbing for apples at that same friend's Halloween party and then me in first grade, crying at my elementary school's haunted house while the people around me removed their costumes to show that they weren't real. I thanked Gabbith for showing me all of these scary moments. I knew she was real because I consciously remembered them as well.

I started to realize that I had to make friends with this part of me if I wanted her to show me what else she had been hiding. It was clear that she wanted to tell me something, but I could feel that she didn't trust me yet. Gabbith didn't like me at first because she didn't like anyone. If she had her way, everyone else would go away. She was carrying a lot of fear and pain and knew about the abuse I had endured when I was four. But she was mad about something even more significant.

In my memories and meditations, I was consistently brought back to a specific place and time—my grandparents' house in Randolph, Massachusetts, in the early '90s. I knew something must have happened to me there, with how consistently I saw this place in my dreams and memories. Over time, things started coming in clearer, sneaking up on me even outside of meditation. Soon, the images appeared in full movies that had me reliving the abuse as if it were happening in real time. The sudden flashes caused a lot of discomfort and made me afraid of my own mind, and I continued questioning what I was seeing, but I was always delivered confirmation of what I was shown in some form or other.

I continued seeing evidence that our bodies don't lie, but they also don't speak our language. They communicate through sensation, pain, shutdowns, flashes of smell or sound, those unexplainable feelings that hit out of nowhere. Reconciliation starts with giving both the mind and the body a seat at the table without demanding that they match up perfectly right away. My nervous system was telling a story I hadn't yet remembered, and I learned to stay curious instead of needing proof. I listened for the cues and asked myself: What does this sensation remind me of? When did it start? What might my body be trying to show me?

It wasn't about solving a mystery overnight; it was about listening, validating, and letting the truth unfold without force. Also, a little pro tip—try not to interrogate your trauma while you're already dysregulated. That would be like trying to defuse a bomb while skydiving. Regulate first, then inquire. Over time, I stopped needing my memories to be logical and started letting my body lead. The body often knows the truth before the mind catches up.

Gabbith began to take over my body often, distraught over what had happened to her and incapable of understanding why no one had saved her. One day, as I watched Uncle Malcolm lure me into a bedroom and do disgusting things to me, I shot up suddenly, noticing someone out of the corner of my four-year-old self's eye. Did he almost get caught? What happened? My mind was going wild.

Oftentimes, new memories like these would cause me to

shoot up out of meditation, run to the bathroom, and dry heave or hysterically cry on the floor. My younger parts were beginning to show themselves in my present reality. Shaking and screaming, I would ask myself why they did this to me. I didn't do anything wrong; I was a good girl! My mom would sit on the floor with me, hugging me and telling me I was safe now. In fact, my experience was occurring *because* I was in a safe place, surrounded by family support that allowed it all to come forth so quickly.

A few days later, Mom and I sat down to have a talk. She asked me if it would be okay for her to call my Uncle Malcolm and tell him that she knew what he had done to me and never to contact the family again. Feeling ready and more grounded than I had been a few months prior, I agreed.

Confronting one's abuser can be emotionally challenging because who in their right mind would admit to having abused someone, let alone their baby niece? I knew I would have loved to hear him admit to it and apologize, but I had to be okay with whatever his response was. Had we tried to do this any earlier, I probably would have done something drastic that I would come to regret. Also, please know, there is no timeline when it comes to confronting one's abuser. If you told them before you felt you were "ready," it's okay. You're not wrong; there's nothing wrong with you. You might not ever feel ready, and that is okay too. You need to do what is best for you without shame or guilt. Some people feel the need, while others don't, which is also fine. But I knew by now that I had the tools I needed to handle whatever outcome arose and cope with however my body felt it needed to react.

So, my parents, brother, sister, and I gathered on the couch on my parents' back porch and hovered around the phone as my mother called Uncle Malcolm. As soon as his voice said hello, my body instantly froze. I could feel his energy in my vagina and was overcome with discomfort, but I hung on, knowing that redemption was on the other side of the conversation. The truth would finally be out, and I wouldn't have to carry it alone anymore—he would finally know that I remembered. I sat frozen, listening to my mother yell that I remembered what he did to me and that he was not to contact this family ever again. As I suspected, her words were met with disbelief and denial. My mother did not want to hear it. She knew the truth and, within a few minutes, she hung up the phone, and the conversation was over.

In spite of his response, the fact that the conversation took place brought us all a feeling of relief. But now we had another task to take care of: telling Uncle Jeremy about the confrontation before Uncle Malcolm could. We tried Jeremy, then Auntie Donna, and eventually my cousins, none of whom answered, which surprised me.

Then, about twenty minutes later, my entire world came crashing down in a way I never would have expected. My personal cell phone rang. It was Uncle Jeremy, with whom I had never spoken privately. It was immediately unsettling. I answered, and he proceeded to tell me he had just gotten off the phone with Uncle Malcolm.

"You'd better watch your mouth, talking like that, or it'll get you in trouble!" he demanded before calling me crazy and saying I needed help.

I dropped the phone and immediately started hyperventilating, hysterically crying, and screaming. Before I knew it, I was thrashing around the house, dry heaving so hard that my parents thought I was having a heart attack.

Finally, my parents managed to calm me down, but I was dysfunctional and confused. What just happened? How could Uncle Jeremy completely flip on me like that? What possessed him to threaten me to keep my mouth shut? Why did I have such a visceral response to him saying he didn't believe me? So many questions were running through my mind, and my family's as well.

That single interaction broke my reality. To this day, I have never had a stronger reaction to anything than I did to those words. But the question was why I was so caught up about these people not believing me when everyone else in my life did? When the answer would finally come to me, it would shatter my reality once again. I had to establish yet more safety and stability within myself before I allowed certain truths to come forward.

Over time, I was continually visited by that memory of Uncle Malcolm on top of me at the foot of my grandfather's bed. It haunted me during the meditations, startling me with a momentary flash and nothing more. Every time, I noticed the door was open and knew someone was about to walk into the room. I was consumed by the feeling that I was on the edge of discovering something really big, but I couldn't see it clearly. For weeks, I watched the scene play across my mind, always in incomplete fragments, disappointed that this mystery person never came in to save me.

More and more, Gabbith was popping up in my present reality. As she took over my physical body, I became like a sad seven-year-old again, screaming and crying out, "Why didn't they save me?" My parents would ask who I was talking about and try to comfort me, telling me that no one had known what had happened to me. Surely, if someone had, they *would* have saved me. Once I calmed down, I would look at them dumbfounded and explain that I had no idea who I was talking about, but the mini dissociative episodes continued.

One day, I was lying down for meditation, getting ready to go to my safe place—the same beautiful spot on the beach I always went to, quiet and magical, where I felt held by something bigger than me. The sound of the waves, the warmth of the sun, and the stillness always brought me peace, but this day felt different. Before I could fully get there, I noticed my body tighten. Something in me knew what was coming even before my mind did.

For the first time, I saw the entire memory play out, clear and complete. It was lunchtime when Uncle Malcolm took me upstairs. I didn't want to go and tried to escape, running to my grandparents' room and hiding in the closet. Uncle Malcolm found me immediately, pulling me out and saying, "You know you need to do what good girls do." I was paralyzed as he laid me down on the bed.

In the corner of my eye, I saw gloomy fall weather outside the window. And then I noticed the door again, left ajar as if someone could come in at any moment. That's when I finally saw Uncle Jeremy walk in and tell him to get off of me. They started arguing, and I shot straight out of the meditation with a racing heart. *He knew all along.*

Little by little, things started clicking off for me. No wonder Uncle Jeremy's first reaction had been to ask what exactly I remembered. When he told me over the phone that I could get in trouble, it was himself he was worried about getting in trouble. But if he knew, why didn't he ever save me? It wouldn't be long before my subconscious mind would deliver me that answer as well. Gabbith was the one holding on to it.

BREAKDOWN AND
THE BRUTAL TRUTH

By June 2017, my life felt like emotional whiplash. One day, I was on the floor sobbing over my past; the next, I was moving through the present like nothing had ever happened. I was learning to ride the waves, lean on the tools I had, use my skills, and do my best to stay present through it all. I started to develop a whole different world, connecting with others online. While I was working through the fears I'd been carrying, the next step naturally revealed itself. I decided that I had been hiding myself for so long and was ready to show myself to the world.

I decided to start a 30-day selfie challenge, where I would post pictures of myself and candidly speak about what I was going through in hopes of helping myself and others feel less alone. I wanted to show that even when people are smiling, we may not be okay. Sharing my experience brought me the thing that I had been desiring—to feel understood and seen. I intuitively knew this would help me, but I didn't realize how much it would benefit those around me. I was entering into the third stage of healing that the trauma therapist had told me about: helping others (naturally, the overachiever inside of me had decided to get a start on the third stage, even if there was still work to do on the first two).

Although I was still struggling internally, things began to look up for me. I was spending a lot of time in nature at one of the hills near my parents' house, where I was still living. I was starting to feel more confident in myself, building more assurance within my internal world as I posted daily photos with captions that included what I was processing and how I was coping—or not coping. I was being brutally honest with the internet, and it felt so good to let it out.

I was still experiencing intense emotions, but I now felt like I had a place to put them. Expressing my true feelings to the world was a liberating feeling that gave me purpose, and I started feeling a little more settled within myself. At first, I was afraid, but I was in my "fuck fear" mindset and quickly embraced the feeling as excitement. I started a blog called "I used to suck at yoga," where I went even deeper into what I was experiencing and the overall struggles I felt as someone who had been through sexual abuse.

As soon as I started telling my story, I was flooded with messages about how refreshing it was to see someone speaking their truth and not hiding behind a mask. People who had been abused and had never told anyone thanked me for being open. On multiple occasions, people who had been contemplating ending their lives told me that my posts gave them hope and made them realize they were not alone. It was the first time in my life that I felt connected to myself and like I was doing the work God had put me on this planet to do. But, like most things in life, with every high comes a low. Skipping to the third step without fully working through the second—or even the first—leaves room for cracks in the foundation.

I already knew that feeling safe to share my memories encouraged my mind and body to show me more. Now, what do you think happened when I began publicly speaking about my experience? Once again, new memories emerged, more graphic and worse than ever. Looking back, I can see how strategic my parts and higher self were with the information they were delivering.

One day, while meditating, I was taken back to the memory of my Uncle Jeremy walking in and yelling at Uncle Malcolm, only to be brought to another memory. This time, it was of Uncle Jeremy, raping me in his bedroom when I was about seven years old, until my aunt walked in and yelled at him to stop. I was in absolute shock and could barely fathom what I had seen, but the memory was so clear, I knew it was true. I was even shown the end of the day, when my dad picked me up. I ran crying down the stairs, and my uncle assured him I just must not be feeling well and had been fine all day.

This memory brought up so much rage within me that I barely knew what to do with myself. The person who could have saved me was also an abuser, and my aunt could have saved me but didn't. So much clicked for me in that moment: the strange reactions when my family and I initially told Uncle Jeremy and Auntie Donna, how Uncle Jeremy had questioned me and Auntie Donna claimed she didn't remember me bleeding as a kid, and that disturbing phone call telling me to watch my mouth.

Not knowing what else to do with my anger, I took it upon myself to write an open letter to them on my blog. I didn't use names—I didn't have to. I wrote what was true: that no one could stop me from remembering, that I knew what had been done to me, and that, in time, others would know too. I wrote about the silence, the complicity, and how turning a blind eye makes you just as accountable.

Within an hour of publishing the post, the phone started ringing nonstop. Uncle Jeremy, who didn't even have social media, somehow found it. He left multiple voicemails, called me crazy, told my parents to get me "under control," and threatened consequences if I didn't stop. He called my dad's cell phone and left more messages with the same tone: fear disguised as aggression.

Shortly after, friends of his I didn't know began leaving comments on the blog, defending him, calling me attention-seeking, insisting he and his wife were "good people." But none of it shook me. In fact, it confirmed everything I already knew. When someone is innocent, they speak. They clarify. They show up. What he gave me was silence. And that silence said more than words ever could. My family had spent months confused about why we hadn't heard from him, and that day gave us all the clarity we needed. We saw it for what it was: not just avoidance, but admission. After that, he disappeared completely. No calls. No visits. Nothing.

I started speaking with members of my extended family and sharing what had happened. Many of them agreed—his reaction was not that of someone falsely accused. It was the response of someone who knew exactly what they had done and had hoped it would stay buried. But the truth doesn't stay buried forever. Not when you're ready to face it.

Through all of this, I continually saw my therapist, described in grave detail exactly what had happened to me, and then questioned once again whether I was just making it up. I was always met with the same response: "Gabriella, look at how your life has been this entire year. This is real." To this day, I still have occasional moments of disbelief, but I know they're just my brain's way of trying to protect me and make me feel like I have some control over the situation.

Once I had processed through a number of childhood memories, I began recovering memories of abuse as a teenager and young adult. Seeing how many predators I had attracted into my life felt surreal. It almost felt like I was somehow at fault for this. I grappled with this for a very long time until I met someone with similar childhood trauma who also translated to abuse as a teenager and adult.

For nearly two years, the pattern continued: a few weeks of peace followed by new, darker memories of abuse. I don't need to allow my shadow to give you every detail of my trauma for you to understand my story. It's important to me, my safety, and the protection of others that I don't share many of the memories spanning from the age of twelve to fifteen. Still, I feel it's important you know some things so that you can see and understand what I attracted and allowed later on in my story.

I came to learn that my aunt was deeply involved with the abuse, and that there were a third and a fourth abuser. I had memories of my uncle's "friend," who would pass me around in a circle in my grandparents' basement. When I was twenty-two, that friend showed up to Thanksgiving dinner, and my Uncle Jeremy proceeded to say slyly, "Oh, you remember him, Gabriella." He also made comments such as, "What, you don't kiss on the mouth anymore?" as I turned my cheek when he tried to kiss me. Now, those strange comments were beginning to make sense.

People often want to believe that women don't get involved in acts like these, and men are often solely demonized. But all types of people can be abusers because people who become abusers tend to be people who were also abused and never dealt with it. That is no excuse for their behavior. In my eyes, these are weak humans who would rather hurt children than face their uncomfortable truths. Predators don't just abuse one child, and abuse is a pattern. Most of the time, children are too scared to speak up, and the pattern continues.

I was often asked why I didn't tell anyone about my abuse, and at first, I didn't understand myself. But then I spent time around three-year-old children and realized that, if you told them the sky was purple, they would agree and take it as truth. Children listen to whatever adults tell them. That's the thing about being a child—you don't know any better yet and are trained to listen to and trust whatever adults tell you to do. So, I understand why it may feel like a harmless question to ask why someone's childhood abuse wasn't reported, but it can be very harmful to the survivor.

Everyone has patterns, and people play them out until they see, heal, and consciously make different choices. Unfortunately, being sexually assaulted by people in positions of trust or authority often continues to play out until we become fully aware of the initial trauma. I carried a lot of shame once I realized this, feeling like everything was my fault and that if only I had remembered everything sooner, I could have prevented the other assaults I experienced.

When we experience abuse in our developing years—whether sexually, mentally, emotionally, physically, or spiritually—we carry an energy that other predators can almost sniff out, like moths drawn to a flame. I refer to this energy as black energy. In my body, I can see it in my solar plexus (the stomach area, where our personal power is) and my sacral chakra (where we hold our sexual energy). Throughout my life, I have mistaken abuse for "normal" behavior because I was an "energetic match" for it.

The unique energies we embody and carry within ourselves are composed of our thoughts, feelings, emotions, ancestors' energies—all the things that have happened to us over our lifetimes. We carry this energy inside of us, and until we become "awake" or "conscious," we continually manifest our reality by this default energy. You don't have to be conscious to manifest; it's something we are always doing. The only difference is the intention behind it.

When we realize we are powerful creators, we can create a vision for our lives, almost like putting a request out to the Universe. Then, it's our job to take the aligned action and trust the divine timing to make these manifestations come to fruition. It's those aligned action steps that help us change our energy into new thought and feeling patterns to then create the things we desire.

It's like becoming a completely different version of yourself; when you're an energetic match to something, it means your dominant thoughts, feelings, and energy align with it.

Here's the catch: you can't think your way into being an energetic match with something because your feelings are what establish the vibrational frequency. In short, we manifest from how our bodies *feel*. Sexual-abuse trauma continually presents itself in very interesting manifestations, day in and day out. This is why healing, releasing the past, learning values, and setting boundaries are essential for survivors.

Having realized I was abused not only by one family member but by at least three other predators, the rage inside me pushed me to a place I could not foresee. Although I continued with my own healing through personal development, EMDR, body sensory motor therapy, and other somatic therapies, I found myself hyper-focusing on revenge for my younger self. I wanted these sick individuals to pay for what they had done to me and others, and I wanted to stop them from doing the same to anyone else. I took this mission very seriously, and the Universe provided.

I swung from one end of the spectrum, completely hiding from myself and others, to the other, sharing exactly what was going on in my life with anyone and everyone. I continued sharing online and also made it a point to integrate my new healing mindset into the fitness classes I was teaching. I would start every class with an intention, telling participants to listen to their bodies and openly explaining that I was making this shift because of my own realizations about suppressed trauma and the effects of complex PTSD. I gave out business cards to those who wanted to follow my journey, which I was referring to as "Turning Pain Into Purpose." I even started a little craft business called "Turning Darkness Into Sparkles," where I sold my creations.

One day after spin class, I received a message from a twenty-three-year-old man who wanted to thank me for being so open and honest. He proceeded to tell me that he didn't know for sure what had happened to me but that he gathered I had been assaulted. His mother had been dealing with this type of PTSD for his entire life as a result of her own childhood trauma and was an advocate for other survivors in the legal sphere. He had just started law school himself and was working with the state governor with the hopes of one day becoming a federal prosecutor to help put the people who robbed his mother of a childhood in jail. Reading the email, my jaw hit the floor. This was most definitely not a coincidence.

Over the next couple of months, I spent significant time getting to know this man, and we developed a friendship. We came from two completely different worlds; he was very well-off, while I was from a middle-class family, yet we had this shared passion of bringing justice to the world of sexual-abuse survivors. He would come over while I did my distress tolerance crafts, and we would talk about a game plan for how I might get justice. His father was also a lawyer, and the family was very well connected in the legal space. They were close friends with two of the lawyers from the case against the Catholic Church, featured in the movie *Spotlight* from two years prior.

Against certain advice I'd received from doctors, my friend encouraged me to pursue legal action. Part of me was afraid, but after my more recent discoveries, I was feeling more ready to actively pursue justice in hopes of not just liberating myself but protecting other potential victims. I took him up on his offer, and he put me in touch with the lawyers.

At that time in my life, while my energy needed to be directed towards me and my own healing, I still sought outside myself for comfort. I didn't quite recognize my own power, that I was the one who would set myself free over time. The Universe had delivered me cream-of-the-crop lawyers to support my desire for justice and revenge, but revenge is not necessarily in one's own best interest or for the highest good. My soul was trying to guide me in a different direction, knowing that my ultimate goal was peace and freedom for myself. I just didn't know how I would get there yet.

I spent extensive time compiling memories and evidence and, shortly after, spoke with both of these top-tier lawyers. They immediately pointed out that because the abuse involved multiple family members and their friends, spanning across years, and starting when I was just a toddler, this seemed like a pedophile ring. It wasn't one isolated incident or one person— it was a pattern of various abusers and settings, all within a connected group of people who had access to me and who likely knew each other. This wasn't just a case of abuse—it was organized, systemic, and bigger than one perpetrator. They couldn't take the case unless I went to the police.

I took this news for what it was. I didn't want to start a civil case against my abusers as it would make it look like I was in it for money, which wasn't at all the point. Going to the police was the last thing I wanted to do—I didn't feel ready, and I was scared shitless—but I knew I had to.

For months, a friend called to ask if I had gone to the police, and I would continually explain that I wasn't ready yet. We sometimes argued as he pushed me to speak with them, but part of me just wouldn't allow me to. Speaking with lawyers who had worked with people like me and built careers around supporting us was one thing. But I did not feel safe with the police, who may not have believed me. I knew that what had happened to me was real—I had validation from myself, therapists, lawyers, and my family, yet I still didn't feel ready to speak it out loud to a police officer.

There's a difference between wanting something and actually going out and doing it. I wanted to pursue justice, but my body didn't feel ready for the "consequences" of doing so. I could feel the fear of my inner child, who felt like she would be in big trouble, that something bad would happen, and it would officially be her fault. It was too much for me to bear, so I pushed it aside, knowing that someday I would go and that I would know exactly when the time was right. I sat with this for quite some time.

In the meantime, my present-day reality was also giving me plenty to deal with. A few days before my twenty-sixth birthday, I received a notification on Instagram from a mystery account with no followers. I'd been tagged in a photo of my boss boyfriend with a blonde girl at a concert. Being genuinely confused about who this girl was and why she had posted this picture and tagged me, I messaged her very politely. To my surprise, she replied, explaining that they had been dating since April, over five months prior, and that he was her boyfriend too. I was beside myself. And, in keeping with how I was living my life at that moment, I yearned for yet more revenge.

Long story short, revenge isn't what I got. What I got was reckoning—a reckoning with the part of myself who still felt like I needed to be chosen in order to be worthy, who thought that love had to come with suffering. In the end, I didn't get the satisfying conclusion. I didn't get the apology. I didn't get the redemption story. I got something better: I walked away. And, this time, I didn't look back.

As you heal, some things must fall away, and this relationship was one of those things. But that's not to say it was easy. Never in my life had I felt more liberated and heartbroken, two feelings I didn't even know could co-exist. I screamed and cried to God, asking what I had done to deserve this. On top of PTSD, I was now also suffering from a painful breakup and unfathomable betrayal. The emotional pain was visceral and inescapably present, a pain I couldn't deny. It wasn't like the memories of abuse, which I could at times attempt to convince myself weren't real. There was no way to deny that this was a real experience, and it highlighted all the heartache I had suppressed for my entire life. I spent my birthday alone at the movies, hysterically crying as I watched *The Glass Castle*, which, of course, turned out to be about running from demons and childhood trauma.

The unexpected event caused me to take a look at what had happened and how I had gotten here. I thought about all the times my boss boyfriend had claimed he would break up with me for things that were helpful for me—like posting certain pictures online, smoking weed, and behaving naturally. These were all things that ended up accelerating my healing, yet I had allowed him to limit my access to them. The way he treated me had felt so normal to me, and I spent years telling myself that these things happen all the time.

Now, I saw that there was a reason behind what had happened. I had been carrying an energy that had attracted this kind of relationship, and he was a predator who knew he could get away with his behavior because of the way that I was willing to mold to whatever he needed me to be in order to receive love. I had dimmed myself down to make him feel comfortable, never wanting to be in trouble. It wasn't my fault, but it was my responsibility to understand how I had been showing up in the world. I had been subconsciously allowing this man to control me all along.

When life feels like it's been turned inside out, that doesn't mean we're failing or broken. When your trauma comes up, it isn't just asking to be fixed—it's demanding to be seen, heard, and integrated. This is the portal. This is how it works. This is the only way we actually wake up.

This incident was a catalyst for me to look out for what I wanted and needed when it came to relationships. I saw that by masking for so long, I had become my own master manipulator. I had tricked myself into thinking that I had been the one in control, but I had been brainwashed by my uncles to such an extent that I eventually brainwashed myself. It was me who had enabled my own relationship dynamics, unknowingly giving my power away to others because that was what felt normal to me.

My boyfriend's betrayal felt like the ultimate wound, and I did not know where to begin to heal it. It wasn't more traumatic than my childhood experiences, but it stirred something deeper, reopening places inside of me that had just begun to feel safe. It wasn't just about what happened. It was about everything it brought to the surface.

My mind couldn't rationalize it. Even after he assured me otherwise, I believed the betrayal might have been because there was something wrong with me. It was almost like my brain felt more in control of the situation if I could just put the blame on myself. At the end of the day, though, if someone betrays you, it says nothing about you and everything about them. He hated himself—he even said so. The external validation had felt good to him. That's a sad and dangerous place, to base your self-worth in what others give you. I could see that now.

My self-love journey was just beginning, but I was grateful to finally be on the path. Instead of seeking approval or validation from others, I was learning to give myself what I used to beg for. It gave me a new lens—one rooted in compassion. I could see how much of what people do to hurt others is really just a projection of their own unhealed pain. And while that didn't excuse the harm, it helped me stop internalizing it.

PART
TWO

PROCESS & INTEGRATION

WHEN GOD WINKS,
YOU LISTEN

During that first year of healing, I spent almost every evening at the gym. It was where I worked, saw my therapist, and swam at night to calm my nervous system. I had made a habit of aqua jogging in the warm pool. On one particular night, I was alone, floating in the water, when an older woman struck up a conversation. I told her that the water helped with my PTSD, and she asked what had caused it, so I told her my story.

She stopped and said, "That happened to me too." She hadn't remembered the abuse until she had children of her own and thought she was losing her mind—until the memories of her grandfather surfaced.

I told her I wanted to help others release the shame of this kind of trauma, and she looked me straight in the eye and said, "You're going to help a lot of people."

"You know that line from Humpty Dumpty?" she asked me. "'All the king's horses and all the king's men couldn't put him back together again.' But you know who could? The king. The king is God. He's the one who can help you heal. Keep listening."

Something about that moment shifted everything. I left the pool feeling stunned, deeply moved. Later in the car, I looked up her name, Ellen. It meant "the light." I started crying. I knew I had just experienced something sacred.

Two weeks later, I saw her again and ran over, excited to say hello. But the woman I thought was Ellen looked at me like I was a stranger, like our interaction never took place. It was as if an angel had worked through her. Some things in life are inexplicable, but when you know, you know.

My whole life, I had this unspeakable connection with something higher than me. My faith was something I was taught but always something I practiced on my own. I grew up going to church every Sunday and was given the choice of whether or not to continue after I was confirmed. I loved going to church because it made me feel that something greater than myself had my back. It was something I had always turned to when I needed it.

When I first remembered what happened to me, my cousin was adamant that I had to give this to God, to forgive and leave it up to him for what would happen. Initially, this didn't sit well with me. How could I just let this go? How could I be so sure God would take care of it? He let it happen in the first place! Ultimately, it didn't make me question my faith in God, but it did make me question why things happen.

Every Sunday, I found myself in a church pew, unable to keep tears from rolling down my cheeks. The Gospel spoke to me, always in parallel with whatever I was experiencing that week. Themes of forgiveness or people not realizing what they do were mapped out onto my waking life. With chills and goosebumps all over my body, I cried in my mother's arms for weeks on end, wondering how they could have done this to me. It had to be for something greater. There had to be an explanation.

My name means "God is my strength," something I've never taken lightly. Some days, I felt strong and full of purpose. Other days, I sank back into victimhood, questioning everything again. But the Universe kept meeting me with God winks, and I made a choice: to use what had happened to me to help others. Everything is divinely orchestrated in order for us to wake up, to remember who we really are, and to see that the power we are seeking outside of ourselves is really within. I don't think I could've moved forward if I hadn't made the decision to use my experiences to help others.

A personal training client told me he hadn't been able to stop thinking about me and how to help me heal. You see, being open with others meant that soon everyone I was interacting with knew I was struggling. He handed me an envelope, and to my surprise, I found five hundred dollars inside. The relationship between trainer and client is so much deeper than just working out. I knew the ins and outs of their lives, holding space for them to vent and grow. Now, I had become the one who was in need of help.

That client also told me that his wife had been having some issues and had seen a past life regression specialist in Newton, a town over from where I lived. He explained that the specialist helped his wife by explaining the pain she was experiencing in her body, though he wasn't sure exactly how. He acknowledged how weird it sounded, but encouraged me to give it a try. I tear-fully thanked him for his kindness and agreed to go.

That night, I went home and researched the specialist. Ross wasn't only a past life regression specialist; he was also a psychic medium and healer. I had never been to see anyone like that before, having believed that psychics were evil people who just wanted to steal money. I didn't understand the nature of timelines or how the spiritual quantum physics world worked, feeling it was against my religion. But I lived under the principle that God forgave, and I was still desperate to try just about anything to get better.

When embarking on the journey of self-discovery, questioning everything you've ever known in your life is part of the process. Trauma survivors in particular have a tendency to use black and white thinking, but it's important to remember that not everything is "bad" or "good." We don't need to agree fully with something for it to contain some truth. It's important to develop the ability to discern for ourselves what to take away from all interactions, leaving behind whatever doesn't resonate. We get to decide what works for us and what doesn't, without pedestalizing or demonizing the source of the energetic exchange. I always get to choose what is true for me.

When the way you think about everything is being transformed, there are times when parts of you come back online and try to convince you that this new way isn't right. It's your job to be the gentle parent who guides these parts of you. Notice them, speak with them, and let them know you understand where they are coming from and that it's safe to be different now. You are in control, and you get to decide what you believe and don't believe.

We live in a world full of choices. May we trust ourselves to make the best choices and honor the fact that we are allowed to change those beliefs at any given time. We are not bound to our own rules and limits. We are all divinely guided and protected; it's our choice whether we want to believe and lean into that or not.

Healing from trauma often requires that we become a completely different version of ourselves—not because we were broken, but because the version of ourselves that developed in survival mode was never the whole truth. Trauma shapes identity. It teaches you who you need to be in order to stay safe, to be loved, to avoid punishment or abandonment. At some point, you might have become the people pleaser, the perfectionist, the overachiever, the one who never needs anything; these roles aren't who you are—they're who you had to become.

When you start to heal, you naturally begin shedding the parts of yourself that were built upon fear. You speak more honestly. You say no. You rest. You trust your body. You stop tolerating what once felt normal. To the outside world—and even to yourself—it can seem like you're becoming a completely different person. But, really, you're just becoming someone who no longer needs to abandon yourself to feel safe. Healing isn't about fixing who you were. It's about remembering who you are underneath it all and choosing to live from that place.

I was ready to be healed and become someone new, so I called Ross. He had told me to prepare three questions I wanted to ask about my future, and we booked an appointment for the following week. Making the appointment, I was willing to completely change every aspect of my life, even the belief system I had been married to for the last twenty-five years.

My client had recommended this because of the body pains and flashbacks I still experienced. I had already seen so many doctors who could not explain what was happening, and part of me felt helpless that this too would be a waste of time. But another part knew there was something more to this. The next week, I drove to Newton, uncertain what to expect but trying to keep an open mind.

Ross explained what we would be doing over the course of the session, and we chatted about what was going on with me. Then, with his help over the next five hours, I worked through multiple past lives, took a peek into the future, looked at my Akashic records, removed entities, channeled my higher self, and learned how to cleanse my energy. I had no idea what half of it meant—I just knew I was supposed to be there. One minute, I was sitting across from a new acquaintance, talking about my sexual trauma like it was a normal Tuesday. The next, I was nodding along as he explained how my past life traumas were showing up in my present-day body as physical pain. Somehow, I stayed. Even weirder, I found myself liking it.

I asked one of the questions about my future: when I would meet my husband. Ross assured me that I would meet him when I was thirty, that we would work in the same field, and that he would help me stay on track with my purpose. This felt good because, since my breakup, I continually found myself sacrificing my own wants and needs in order to please whomever I was dating. Maybe it was the trauma, or maybe it was just part of the human experience and the desire to feel love.

Whether consciously or not, we often search for someone to come and give us the love we believe will be the thing to finally heal us. For so long, regardless of what was going on, all I cared about was finding my future partner. I craved it so much that it wasn't until halfway through my thirtieth year on earth that I realized I wasn't going to sacrifice who I was or what I wanted from a life partner.

I look back at my younger self and see all the energy I was using to find someone else that I could have been pouring back into myself, but we often look for love in another person before we learn that giving it to ourselves is what helps us attract the right partner. When the right partner comes along, it's just as easy to pour into ourselves as it is to them—a mutual giving and receiving of something sacred that feels like home.

I also asked Ross about my long-term career. He told me that he saw me writing a one-woman show called "My Body." I'm just going to leave that right here and let us all see how it plays out.

During the healing part of our session, Ross introduced me to my higher self, the part that's connected to infinite intelligence and guides us in the direction of our highest good, always looking out for us. It's there to access whenever we please.

Granted, I took a lot of what he shared with a grain of salt. I wasn't fully sold on the whole woo-woo thing, but I could feel there was truth behind it. Ross's own wife wasn't fully onboard with his beliefs, but he told me she always felt better after the energetic cleansing he performed before they went to bed at night. It was interesting to hear that, regardless of someone's beliefs, the effects can still be felt.

Whether I consciously knew it or not, at this stage in my journey, I was still holding onto my abuse for the life of me. Even though I felt ready to become my new healed self, I still heavily identified with my trauma. To stop carrying the abuse seemed like an impossible task. For some survivors, past life regression helps them release their trauma completely. But for me, even as I did my healing work, I sensed there was something more. This wasn't just about personal release—it was about purpose. I felt it in my bones. I wasn't here just to let go of what had happened. I was here to expose it. To break the cycle. This felt bigger than me—it still does.

Much of what he explained I had already perceived to some extent in meditation and self-hypnosis. I didn't find any relief in analyzing my past lives to explain the severe traumas of my present life. For some people, studying past lives is easier than grasping and processing what has actually happened in their present lives, almost like a gateway to work through their experiences. To me, those lives were over, and the only thing I cared about was the here and now. But I didn't let this bother me. No approach is right or wrong; they are just different perspectives. I got to choose what to energetically take on.

At the end of the session, Ross told me to close my eyes and asked if I saw any dots behind my eyelids. He explained that these were entities, negative energies that come into our field from various places and lives. I remembered being young and closing my eyes at night, talking to the dots that danced around my eyelids like a little light show. So many things that had always seemed unremarkable were coming to take on deeper meaning, the more I healed. We cleared out these entities together until, for the first time in my life, I saw complete darkness when I closed my eyes.

The session allowed me to add more practices to my toolbox. I could do these cleansings and clearings whenever I was feeling off. All I had to do was call on my angels, archangels, spirit guides, higher self—whatever I felt most comfortable with, and they could come down and assist me. I had the power in my own mind to do this on my own, and I didn't need the help of anyone else. I left that day feeling lighter and clearer in a way that I couldn't really describe.

My session with Ross opened the door to a lot that I still wasn't able to rationalize. I was seeking healing but still didn't know that healing was in the living. But now I saw that for my whole life, I hadn't been able to feel energy because I had been so out of tune with my body, clouded and robbed of my body connection after the trauma I had endured.

Now, I saw energy differently. If everything really is energy and we are always creating from what we know in our energy bodies, then, of course, past lives can connect to the present body. Everything is connected, and we can't have our present lives without our pasts. It's all about whether we're willing to go within and heal.

When it comes to trauma and abuse, no spiritual context can negate the pain and suffering the parts of us feel in our present-day body and experience. It can be extremely harmful to the psyche to say things like, "I chose this" or "I did something bad in a past life; I deserve what happened to me." Our ego plays some tricky games in order to feel in control of a situation that we were completely powerless in as innocent children.

It's not always about finding the deeper meaning or cosmic lesson behind unexplainable circumstances. It becomes very easy to use spirituality as a way to bypass what's really happening in your life and in your own body, but some things don't offer clarity—they offer awe. The lines can blur when you look at things from an esoteric lens, and it's important to remain grounded in the here and now. I've learned to let those moments be what they are without needing to wrap them in explanation.

One day, I messaged Cassie, a former boss of mine, and she told me she had since become a life coach. I shared that I was interested in that career path but that I needed to get my head on straight from the PTSD I was still processing. In spite of all of the psychological tools I now had under my belt, I was still struggling with my mental health and body so much that I could barely function in the real world. There was no work I felt comfortable doing full-time outside of the house, and even though I was living with my parents, I bore the financial burden of student loans, car payments, and regular therapy. I was still seeking any help I could find to get better and reconnect my mind and body, and she offered me a free session with her.

I couldn't believe I was resorting to life coaching with someone who wasn't even trauma-informed, but I was so fed up with trauma doctors and feeling let down by the mental health system. We in America pay all this money for health insurance under the assumption that if something happens to us, the resources we need will be available, but that was not my experience. What I was experiencing was still so severe, and I was stunned by the shortage of resources and doctors who were actually willing to help me.

After my free session with Cassie, I decided it was something I needed to continue, though I had no idea how I was going to pay for it. We worked together once a week, which helped me feel more in control of my circumstances and stay on track with my goals. At the end of our three-month container, she told me she was training and certifying others and asked if I was interested in taking the journey to becoming a coach myself.

I didn't quite know what to expect, but I knew in my heart that this step would allow me to help more people, so I eagerly agreed. The certification started out with distinguishing why we wanted to become a coach and writing out our vision for ourselves. I had a dream of starting a trauma foundation, writing a book, and being a public speaker all over the world. My initial vision was to be "the next Oprah," as she had come out about her own sexual trauma, and I had felt very inspired by her story. I wanted to help people not feel alone and give them the guidance they would need on their journey. I was essentially looking to become the person I had needed when I first remembered my trauma, the person I still needed a year and a half later (there I was again, skipping ahead to stage three of trauma recovery!).

I was given a list of books that I would need to complete for the certification. *The Big Leap* by Gay Hendricks opened my eyes to where I was using my energy and how I could learn to master my gifts in order to benefit myself and others. The term "upper limit problems" stood out to me, explaining how, when people reach their goals, they often sabotage themselves because they don't feel worthy due to underlying trauma, a pattern I found familiar. Another book reintroduced the concept of the higher self, explaining it as who we are without any fear, the part of ourselves that is most connected to our true selves. What would I do if I had no fear? Once I opened the door to this knowledge, I couldn't close it. I was obsessed with learning more, leveling up, and trying to become the best version of myself.

For a month, I had been building my relationship with my higher self through daily meditations, journal prompts, and tasks that embodied this connection. I visualized her, about thirty years old and often wearing teal or purple, with long brown hair and a beautiful smile. I meditated on childhood memories, and she brought clarity and helped heal the past. I started to refer to her as the Good Witch and to the parts of me as the munchkins, Dorothy, the tin man, the scarecrow, and the lion, bringing them all together to make the best decision for me and my highest good. I really enjoyed this portion of the training, as I had already been deep in parts work and found it helpful to view my psyche like this.

On one occasion, I was supposed to dress up as and act like my higher self and do the things she would do. I was visiting my friend Mel in Cape Cod that day, which meant driving through other cities in Massachusetts. Typically, I couldn't even drive through the towns where I had been abused without excruciating body pains. I tended to avoid these places, knowing that the pain was often so intense that I would have to pull over.

On my way back home from the Cape, dressed up as my higher self, I decided to roll the dice and drive home the shorter way, knowing I would see the signs for Taunton and Randolph. But my higher self had no fear, and no one had control over her. As I was about to approach the Taunton exit, a crazy thought came to me.

It had been almost a year since I had spoken with the lawyers who told me that I needed to report the abuse before we could pursue a lawsuit against my abusers. I took a deep breath and asked my higher self and God to give me a sign that I was ready. I picked up my phone, put my music on shuffle, and "Beautiful Crazy" by Luke Combs came on. It was the song I had chosen to represent my higher self. I got full-body chills and drove straight to the police station in Taunton without telling a soul. It was finally time to report what had happened to me.

MAGIC AND
THE MESSY MIDDLE

When I sat down with the detective and police officer and told them about the abuse, they believed me and instructed me to inform the Randolph police station as well. I did just that and continued home, feeling freer and prouder of myself than I had in my entire life. Back in the car, I called my parents, who were in shock. After months of offering to come with me to make the report, my higher self and I did it all on our own.

It was the first time I could remember leaning into trusting myself and knowing that I had the power and the answers within myself, regardless of what may have happened in the past and what the voices in my head were telling me. Everyone else was just as proud as I was, which only validated how right it felt. Yet this opened another door that I did not foresee. Oh, how the pieces come together when you let go and let God.

After I went to the police, I started to feel a new sense of power. It was a foreign feeling after the emotional lows that had dominated the prior year and a half. The next few weeks were filled with more conversations with the detective, including with other people in my life as they were summoned to the police station to go on record about the situation. Although I knew this would be a taxing process, I felt a sense of relief in knowing I had done what the lawyers had told me to do. Now, I would finally be able to pursue legal action—or at least that's what I thought.

By the end of September 2018, I was working out every day, working on my life coaching certification, meditating, going to therapy multiple times a week, posting about my journey online, and continually building my relationship with my higher self and listening to her guidance. But, still, something felt like it was missing.

By this point, I had built several relationships with other mental health activists and was speaking with them online on a daily basis. One individual in particular, Jerome, had a brand called "All Grateful and Shit." Though our journeys were very different, we bonded over our shared desire to help others.

That summer, Jerome had sent me some merchandise, and one day he suggested I come out to LA, where he was, explaining that there were lots of opportunities there to help young kids. But I had no idea how I would get to Los Angeles; I was just scraping by as it was. He encouraged me to check it out regardless, assuring me that there was a lot of work for me to do there and that he just knew it would be good for me.

Other than a dream of becoming a surfer and living in California for its beautiful beaches, I didn't really know much about LA. Sitting cross-legged on the gym's green turf in between sets of kettlebell swings, I felt sick of the disgusting, rainy weather and told Jerome I would think about it.

The next day, I told Cassie about the conversation in our life coaching session. She gasped and said she was moving there the following week and had been trying to find someone to drive across the country with her and her dogs, not wanting to do it alone. She offered to take me with her. All I had to do was take the train to New York to meet her.

It was only a few months prior that I had begun learning about and tapping into my higher self and higher wisdom. The practice put me in a state of peace, bliss, and receptivity to whatever I was told. It finally felt possible to me that I was going to do something big in this world. So, when this chance presented itself, it couldn't have been more perfect—another God wink, for sure. I could drive with her, check it out for a few days, and then fly back after. No harm, no foul. What I didn't know was that the journey would spark the biggest spiritual awakening I had ever had.

There's a brutal, almost cliché truth here: Trauma and spiritual awakenings are linked. Most people don't talk about it, or they wrap it up in pretty language and pretend healing is always peaceful. It isn't. When old pain starts breaking through, it can feel like your life is falling apart. But this is often how real awakening begins—not through meditation cushions and incense, but through chaos, breakdown, and raw survival.

What I didn't realize then was that the real work of healing hadn't even started. I was about to get hit with everything I hadn't fully faced, and it would force me to wake up in ways I had never imagined. Even after all of this time of looking at my trauma, I didn't quite understand how I hadn't yet dealt with the severity of it all. Soon, it would all replay in my present life, right before my eyes.

As soon as I stepped foot on the train to New York, I felt a great wave of excitement. I knew something good was going to come from this; I just wasn't sure what it was exactly. A few hours later, we were all on the road—me, Cassie, and her two dogs. It had been four years since we'd seen each other in person, and the first couple of hours of the trip were spent catching up on our lives outside of our coaching sessions. We both were surprised at how well this had turned out and excited for the new journey across the country together.

Though I was becoming more connected to myself and my body again, I was still highly medicated. My psychiatrist had continued to increase my doses, even as she reminded me that no medication could truly help me. Simultaneously, I was stoned for most of the day, as weed was the only thing that seemed to keep my brain from going to the past. I was learning to listen to my higher self, but I was constantly dissociating, numb to energies and feelings. So often, we unconsciously give our power away when we are seeking answers. Sometimes, our own wants and desires can override the truth.

Never in my life had I noticed repeating numbers (other than 11:11, which I had always deemed a meaningless coincidence), but on that first day of the drive, I saw the numbers 444 seemingly everywhere I looked. Cassie explained that the spiritual meaning behind this was that my angels were looking out for me. I viewed her as a wealth of knowledge and trusted her perspective, and the thought excited me and validated my decision to embark on this journey.

One of the first stops on our road trip was to a psychic in a little town in New York. It wasn't really my thing, but I went along with it. After all, I was learning how to become a coach, and my coach wanted to do this, so it had to be the right thing to do. The psychic told me she kept seeing my name everywhere—all over billboards, park benches, buses. I didn't make too much of it but continued listening. Next, she channeled my grandfather and a friend of mine who had died when I was in elementary school. Due to the nature of the things she was saying about them, I truly felt like it was real, and the experience put me in a more open mindset to the spiritual experiences I was already having.

Over the next week, Cassie and I brainstormed ideas of how we could work together. She had a vision of creating a collective of people to coach and felt confident that she wanted to work with me to do so. I trusted her and her expertise, and it felt great for me and my potential to be acknowledged by someone I was learning from. Cassie would teach me everything, and I would be her assistant and help her get this thing off the ground.

The only place we intentionally spent time in instead of just passing through was Sedona, Arizona. We visited several crystal shops and hiked to one of the vortexes. These geological and metaphysical phenomena are believed to hold unique energetic properties and are associated with spiritual and healing experiences. It was a concept I was unfamiliar with, and I was excited to hear that the vortex would bring out energy inside of me that needed to be healed.

These vortexes are often found at specific locations within Sedona's striking red rock formations, and people visit them to connect with the energies they believe exist at these sites, often engaging in practices like meditation, yoga, or simply appreciating the natural beauty of the area. We hiked to one of them, and when we arrived, I decided to meditate. In my meditation, I was met with my mother wound—at its core, the emotional pain, unmet needs, and psychological patterns we carry from our relationship with our mothers or primary female caregivers. It can look like low self-worth, difficulty trusting, people pleasing, perfectionism, or a constant search for validation. For some, it comes from neglect or emotional absence. For others, it might stem from overprotection, enmeshment, or even abuse. It's not about blaming our mothers. It's about acknowledging how early relationships shape the nervous system and the way we relate to love, safety, and ourselves.

These dynamics often pass down through generations, as mothers who were wounded themselves do the best they can with what they have. For me, understanding the mother wound wasn't an intellectual realization—it was a felt one. I had to grieve the protection I didn't have and the parts of myself I had abandoned just to stay connected. It took time, space, and a lot of inner reparenting to start separating my worth from someone else's ability to protect me.

I knew that I had been harboring resentment toward my mother about what had happened to me. Even though deep down I knew that it wasn't her fault, I still found myself lashing out at her and blaming her for what her family members did to me. Prior to going to the vortex, this felt justified, especially to my inner child. It was a way for me to take my anger out on someone other than myself.

That day, I sat on the ground crying, grieving the pain I felt and knew my mother felt for me. Naming the mother wound gave me a kind of permission: to feel what I was never allowed to feel, to see myself more clearly, and to begin writing a new story—one that wasn't defined by the past, but informed by it. It was a powerful experience I could not have foreseen, and I felt so cleansed after.

When we were done at the vortex, we decided to go to a crystal shop. I spotted a crystal necklace I liked and asked the shop employee what the stone's meaning was. It was a crystal to help heal the mother wound, she told me. Goosebumps covered my body, and I cried again, knowing that this was no coincidence and that I was stepping into something bigger than myself. All of the magical things that were happening felt like signs that this trip was pushing me toward my greater purpose.

While it was one of the most magical times of my life, it was also one of the most traumatizing, though that would take me a long time to unpack. When we finally arrived in LA, the plan was for me to stay a week or so with Cassie before figuring out where I would stay after that. I had a limited budget and limited income, but I was going to make it work. So, I spent the next couple of weeks in and out of short-term rentals, spending all my money on rental cars, food, and places to live until I completely ran out. After I slept in my car for a night—which Cassie told me was a test of a good life coach, an initiation everyone had to go through—she decided that I could stay with her until we found a place where we could both live together. I moved to the couch in the porch area of her back room, which was just fine with me. Being in California, I felt better than I had in almost two years, and I was just happy to still be there. In fact, I decided I would settle there longer term.

For the holidays, I flew back to Boston, packed up my things, and shipped my car to start my new life in California. This decision felt like a very bold statement, not only to the Universe but to everyone around me. For the first time in my life, I felt like I was finally choosing myself.

It didn't necessarily go over well—with anyone in my life. A dear friend of mine felt like I wasn't acting like myself, a response I wasn't happy with. Couldn't others see I had finally found a way out of all the emotional distress I was in? How could anyone not support this decision?

My parents were happy I had found something that brought me relief, but they were genuinely confused and concerned. I could barely pay my bills as it was, and now I was just going to up and move across the country? But I had made up my mind. Cassie kept telling me I was making the right decisions, and I trusted my life coach. This was where I was going to live, and I was going to start this business.

When I returned to LA, Cassie and I finally made a plan to move into a short-term rental together until we found an apartment where we could sign a lease. I barely had any money, but she agreed to take care of everything until our business took off and had the funds to pay her back. In my body, I didn't feel comfortable with this arrangement, yet I allowed myself to override the doubts, continuing to think that she knew better than me. She always encouraged me to have faith, and I knew I didn't want to turn my back on faith.

For the next month and a half, we worked on her project, practicing coaching and searching for a new space. We eventually landed an apartment right by the beach in Marina Del Rey. It was way beyond my budget, but she encouraged me that it would be fine and that I would be able to do it. We spent countless hours together, day after day, building this so-called business. In reality, most of the work meant me filming videos for her coaching brand or helping out with whatever project she was chasing at the time.

When we are working through deep emotional trauma, desperate to find the cure and get better, this energetic state opens us up for others to swoop in and potentially hurt us. These people might not even mean to hurt us, but we can get caught in the crossfire when we are shifting from one new reality to the next. I felt I was learning and didn't question it, but the truth is, I had no clue how to navigate my new spiritual reality and merely defaulted to her lead. I handed over my power without even realizing it, doing whatever she wanted and letting her opinions shape every move I made.

Sometimes things come with a warning label; unfortunately, this was not one of them. I was so caught up in what I thought she was doing that I missed the obvious: I was actually the one with a bigger platform, who was already helping people—just by telling the truth about my life. I was making an impact, for free, while she was out there projecting her own unprocessed trauma and calling it guidance. But I wasn't really present. I was too distracted by comparing myself, too wrapped up in what everyone else was doing, and, honestly, still avoiding some hard truths of my own. It's easy to spot someone else's avoidance when you're ignoring your own.

As the days went by, my anxiety climbed through the roof. I had been working tirelessly on my mindset, yet, no matter what I did, my body was still being triggered into the past and my unprocessed trauma. It's not that I wasn't dealing with the trauma—I was looking at it and experiencing it head-on—but I still wasn't able to rid it from my body.

I had spent a year and a half learning to cope but not necessarily learning to process and release. In that state, my life became extremely chaotic. Living with Cassie's dogs was getting to me. As a kid, I was wired to believe that animals weren't safe. Part of me was still scared of them because of trauma I hadn't dealt with—like the time my uncle locked me in a kennel or how Uncle Malcolm's house was always overflowing with animals. My body was in panic mode, and I had no idea how to handle it.

When I couldn't take it anymore, I decided to reach out to a friend's uncle, who lived in Las Vegas and had told me to give him a call if I ever ended up on the West Coast. When we first met, we bonded over God, and he encouraged me to move to California, insisting that life was easier and calmer over there, especially for someone with my life experiences. He had reassured me that I would get better, but there I was, still dealing with PTSD after three months of living in California, freaking out and not knowing what to do. When I called him, he said it sounded like I needed a break and booked me a trip to visit him.

The more conscious I became over time, the more I started to notice the Universe delivering me what I like to call "corrective experiences." Corrective experiences are always showing up in our lives. They can be found in the patterns we repeat until we "heal" them, like loose ends being tied up as we learn to create from our higher self rather than from our trauma. It's up to us to notice when we are stuck in a pattern and to make different choices than we would if we were in survival mode. I was about to encounter one of my first corrective experiences from the Universe.

Previously in my life, older male figures often either wanted something from me or took advantage of me sexually. This was the first time God sent me one who had my best interests at heart and wanted to help me heal. He flew me down to Vegas, put me up in a beautiful hotel, and handed me a stack of money to do whatever I wanted with for the next three days. No one had ever done anything like that for me, and I was genuinely confused. He insisted that God had told him to do it and that it was important for me to receive it. But I didn't know how to. I didn't feel worthy of being blessed in that way. For the first time in my life, I was experiencing what it was like to receive something without any attachment to needing to give anything back.

Although the Universe was providing me with corrective experiences, I was unable to see things clearly. I was still wearing my trauma goggles. They were wiped cleaner and cleaner over time, but I had yet to really look at my deeper wounds. I accepted his generosity, but I couldn't bring myself to spend the money. I just held onto it, frozen. My anxiety didn't go away. If anything, I felt more on edge—like I didn't know how to let myself receive or enjoy any of it.

But I was there, so I was going to make the best of it in the ways I was able to. He was a very spiritually attuned person in spite of a tough exterior, and we discussed all kinds of spiritual things. He said he wanted to help me and that I didn't have to live with so much pain. Some part of me didn't receive this input well; I was so enmeshed in the pain that I viscerally experienced every single day in my body, mind, and spirit. I listened, though, as he explained that he had worked with a lot of women who had gone through similar experiences. What people like me needed to heal, he believed, was ayahuasca and mushrooms. He felt deeply that this was what I needed and offered to find someone to guide me through a ceremony if I wanted.

The only plant medicine I had experienced was marijuana, which I had only started smoking the year prior—and, even that, I had been reluctant to try. Ayahuasca, on the other hand, scared the living shit out of me. Not only that, but I would need to come off all of my medications, which was something entirely outside the realm of possibility for me. I explained my hesitations, and he told me that when I was ready, he would be there and so would the medicine. In the meantime, I would be left to do the same thing I had been doing: solely coping with my symptoms while figuring out how to navigate the decision of uprooting my life to California.

Back in LA, I was very active on social media, posting four times a day and building my own brand. As I continued sharing my story with others, lots of opportunities were coming my way. Every time I was asked to speak or write an article, though, it seemed that Cassie's response was to ask if I had consulted her about it. Confused, I would say no, explaining that the topics I was speaking on didn't really have to do with her or the spiritual aspects of business that she was focused on. She was my life coach, sure, but the trauma portion of stuff I was working on had always been a separate thing. What always seemed to follow was an angry or resentful response.

In January, Cassie decided to leave for three weeks, putting me in charge of her two untrained dogs. They tore through the house, barking constantly and pooping everywhere. Every time I brought up how stressful it was or asked for advice, she gave a nonchalant, spiritual response. "Just see it as a gift from God," she would say, brushing me off. There was never any acknowledgment of my stress or discomfort; only her perspective mattered.

Looking back, I can see this wasn't really about the dogs. It was about control and invalidation. My coach made everything about her, dismissed my feelings, and twisted every challenge into some kind of spiritual lesson that only served her. My reality didn't matter—my job was to manage her chaos and keep her world running, no matter how I felt. And, typically, instead of speaking up or setting boundaries, I stayed quiet and kept the peace, reminding myself that she knew better. It was like my needs were invisible, my discomfort ignored, and I was just expected to fall in line.

A woman named Kerilyn, a mom in her forties, had somehow found me online and been following my journey. I hopped on a call with her and told her about everything I was experiencing—how Cassie always made everything about herself, dismissed my feelings, showed no real empathy for what I was going through, constantly crossed my boundaries, and twisted situations to make herself look wise while I was left to deal with the mess. Something about Kerilyn made me feel comfortable with her, and I poured my heart out to her. She told me she had experienced an abusive narcissistic relationship and that that's what she thought I was dealing with. She urged me to remove myself from the situation and offered to help me create an escape plan.

Over the three weeks while Cassie was away, I mentally

and physically prepared myself to leave the apartment. I was beside myself and practically dysfunctional with all kinds of emotions running through me. I felt confused and guilty about what I was about to do, going back and forth in my head about whether it was the right decision. Was I just being crazy? I liked my coach and had felt very connected to her at times, but my body was telling me otherwise.

The day before I was set to leave, I received a random package in the mail from a publishing company. I hadn't ordered anything and wasn't expecting any mail, so I opened the box with curiosity. Inside was a book by Jackson MacKenzie, called *Whole Again: Healing Your Heart and Rediscovering Your True Self After Toxic Relationships and Emotional Abuse*. I started reading it that night and realized it was describing exactly what I was going through. I began to consider that maybe I wasn't crazy; I had just found myself in yet another position of being abused. This was exactly the sign I needed to know that leaving was the right decision.

The day my coach was supposed to come back from her trip, I fed the dogs and left a note explaining that this wasn't working for me anymore. I even used her own language, saying I got a "hit" that I needed to leave for both of our sakes. Then, I packed my things, went to stay with our assistant, and never looked back.

There are parts of me that blamed myself for everything that had occurred, yet a stronger part of me knew that you can't know something until you see it clearly. Sometimes, only by having the experiences we have and trusting the process are we able to see things clearly. Regardless, it took me a long time to retrieve the part of myself I lost along this portion of my journey. I felt ridden with shame, thinking I should have known better and blaming myself for the choices I had made. In reality, I was only doing the best I could at that point in my life. I *didn't* know better; I was dealing with severe PTSD.

It's important for me to note that I also don't blame my coach for this situation. Rather, I am calling out a paradigm. Like many other trauma survivors, I was seeking direction and healing during my time of spiritual awakening and made a lot of choices that felt right to me at the moment. Healers and coaches are often forthright and very willing to help, maybe even for free, and it's important to proceed with caution when it comes to working with someone with that kind of influence. I thought I was doing what was best for me, but there was a piece of the puzzle I had not figured out yet: self-trust, a simple yet intricate concept.

When you're abused as a child by someone you were told loves you, there is an immediate disconnect from your true self—the part of you that feels safe and knows that everything is happening for you. I was so disconnected from this part of myself that I didn't start completely trusting myself until years after this chapter of my life. I had looked at a lot of my wounds, but I had not fully unpacked others. My inability to see them caused a lot of chaos.

It took me a long time to make peace with my decision. I spent so many days afraid my coach would come after me or try to hurt me, and my inner child was constantly bracing for danger, even when it wasn't there. When I got that message from Kerilyn, though, something in me knew to trust it, a choice that changed everything. It was the catalyst for a lesson I didn't expect or want to learn at the time, but it was something

I needed in the end. For the first time, I had truly trusted myself when I had absolutely everything to lose from it.

We're going for progress—not perfection—on this journey, and I hope you are able to find the humor through the horrors of this experience. As we know and have repeatedly seen throughout this book, it's always both.

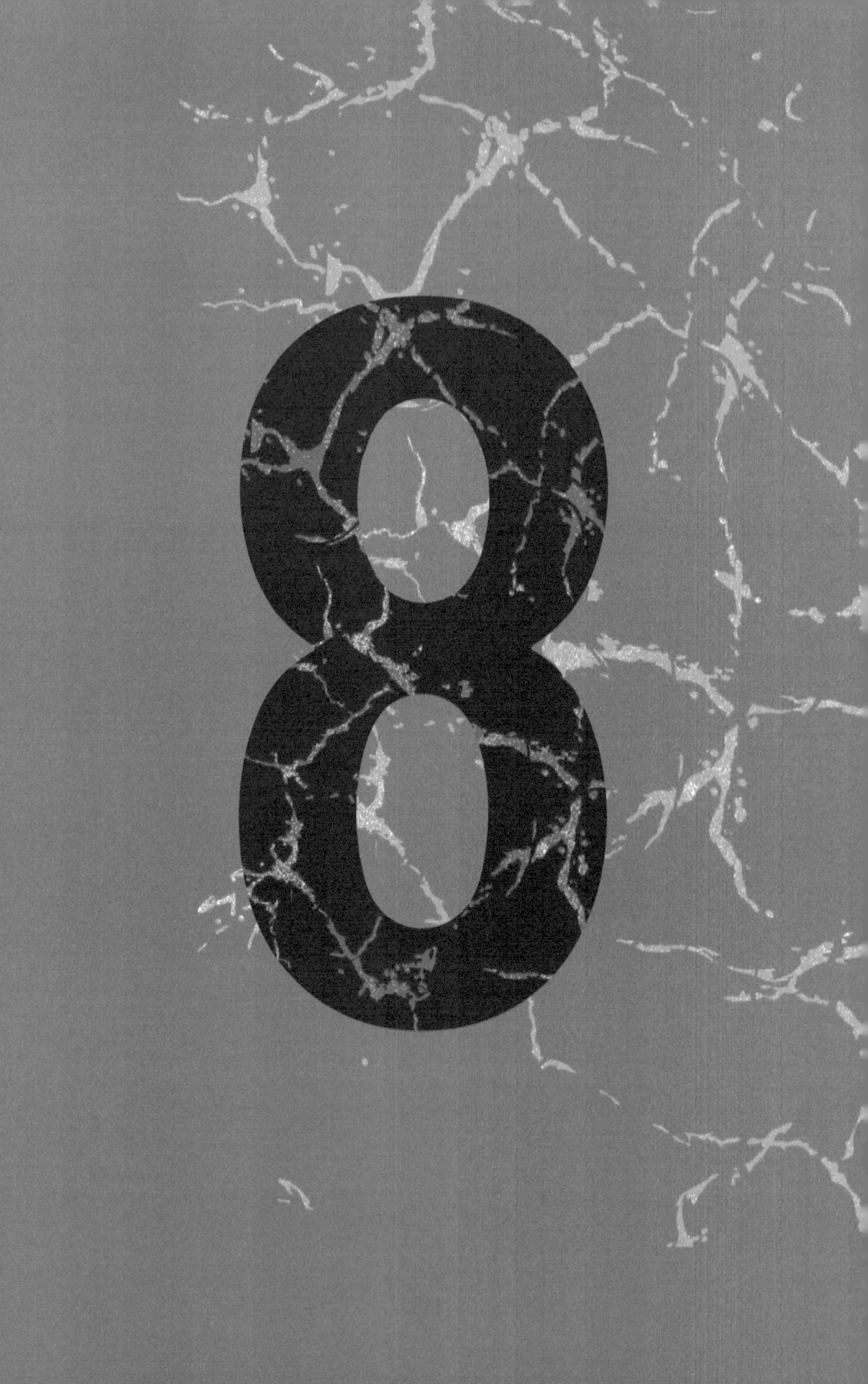

MAKING PEACE WITH THE PIECES

For the first four years of my healing journey, I spent a lot of time feeling soul-crushingly lonely. I had poured out my heart and soul online, sharing the depths of my mental health journey. And while I *knew* it was helping others—and, honestly, helping me too—I still felt this deep, gnawing shame around how exposed I had made myself. It wasn't that I regretted being honest, but something shifted when I realized that people were starting to *feel bad* for me. That was never my intention. I wasn't trying to be pitied—I was trying to be understood.

What caught me off guard was this quiet heartbreak: As more people read my story, I could *feel* how deeply they were affected by what I had been through. Yet, no one close to me reached out. No one checked in. No one said, "Hey, I read what you shared—how are you really doing?" And a part of me started to wonder: *If they felt that bad, why didn't they say anything? Why didn't anyone stop me from unraveling so publicly?* My higher self understood—they likely just didn't know how to hold it. But the other parts of me felt abandoned, unseen, and deeply alone.

It didn't matter where I was, who I was with, or if anyone else could relate to me; I still felt this overwhelmingly burdensome feeling of being alone. I would go to parties, gatherings, meetings with friends, but I always had this empty pain inside, as if my heart was completely broken. I would try to vocalize this to others, but I was always met with words like, "You're not alone" or "There are so many others who have gone through abuse like you have. You don't have to feel this way." The responses may have been well-intentioned, but they made me feel even more lonely and broken inside. I was so overwhelmed by the sadness I had repressed over the years that I couldn't cope with it anymore.

So often, we repress the parts of ourselves that we believe to be wrong or bad. What if these parts of us are really just trying to protect us? Sometimes, they're just doing their best to shield us from pain—even if their methods are messy or misguided. They act out because they believe that's the only way to keep us safe.

It wasn't until I started sitting with the parts of me that were sad that this loneliness started to let up. They would show up in sneaky ways, like robbing me of my ability to write or go about my daily life, until I would take the time to speak with them and hear them out. Once I realized this, I started intentionally allowing those parts of me to fully express themselves through my body.

After spending so much time hating them and wanting to get rid of them, I became friends with them. I learned that all they were looking for was to be seen, heard, and loved. I started doing what I like to call a "team meeting," where I would get comfortable in my bed, put on some meditation music, and visualize all the parts of me sitting at a table in my head. I would allow them to speak their truth one by one, asking them what they needed in that moment or what they required me to do for them to give me back control of my body. My inner child would often ask for ice cream, while my inner teenager just wanted to go boxing and let out some aggression.

Over time, I developed a system where I would allow each part of myself to express herself for a day. One day, I'd allow my inner child to run the show, dressing however she wanted, wearing my hair in pigtails—you name it, I gave it to her. Another time, my inner teenager, Gabby, expressed that she was very confused about what my life had become. She was from a place where everyone knew everything about each other and barely anyone ever left. I had broken away from that life, which wasn't what she felt should be happening. Once you are aware of your patterns and the patterns around you, you can break free of anything you put your mind to, but even after you break away, it's still completely normal to have doubts.

Sometimes, it's not so easy to recognize when another part of you has "taken the wheel," as I like to call it. In August, right around my birthday, Gabby showed up and took over my experience. For two weeks, I felt stuck, not acting like myself, unable to write, and feeling frustrated with life and where I was at. Multiple times, I sat on the couch scrolling through Instagram and looking at people from my hometown. As I did so, I cried about feeling like an outsider, even going as far as thinking my parents were disappointed in me for taking a different path than everyone else we knew, which was far from the truth.

One day during meditation, Gabby finally presented herself. I asked her what was going on and how I could help her. She said she felt like such a loser for speaking up about her trauma and spiritual awakening and that she felt so misunderstood by the people she grew up with. She didn't want to write this book; she just wanted to go back to her hometown and be normal so that people could understand her again.

Kindly and gently, I explained that not everyone would be willing to understand her, and that writing this book would be the very thing that would help her be understood by those who were willing. She still had some reservations and asked if I thought people would judge me for what I was exposing about myself, and I comforted her. Even if they did judge me, it was okay because we already had an entirely new life and so many people who already loved and supported us. "I'm thirty-two now, and I'm safe," I told her. Within a few minutes, I heard her careful reply: "Okay, I trust you. I love you. Let's keep writing." I felt the shackles she had placed on me release, and my ability to write came back instantly.

The years we spend growing up—especially in childhood and adolescence—are foundational. They're where we begin to form our sense of self, our beliefs about the world, and our understanding of love, safety, and belonging. What we see, how people treat us, and even *why* they treat us that way don't just shape our personalities—they imprint our nervous systems. These early experiences don't exist in a vacuum. They're influenced by family dynamics, cultural expectations, generational patterns, and systemic influences—what some might call *societal trauma*. And, unless we become conscious of these imprints as adults, we can end up repeating the very cycles that hurt us without even realizing it. The thread doesn't break just because we grow older. It breaks when we decide to *see* it. When we choose to ask, *Is this really mine?* and *Do I want to carry this forward?* That's where the real healing begins.

If you're experiencing parts of yourself in this way, I encourage you to be the gentle observer of them and their requests. Even if you don't agree with them, hear them out and ask what they really want. You see, my inner teenager didn't necessarily want to keep me from sharing myself; deeper than that was her desire to feel seen and heard. It is my adult self's job to find a way to integrate her experience without belittling the way she feels. Once I allowed these parts of me to be present with me and see that I was safe, they learned to trust me enough to integrate into my body. That was when they stopped trying to protect me from the danger they had perceived.

Once I became a coach, I noticed that many people were aware of their inner child, but most got stuck on their inner teenager. If you're feeling disconnected from your inner teenager, there are gentle ways to start building a relationship with them. Begin by sitting in stillness, closing your eyes, and imagining them in front of you. Ask simple, open-hearted questions like, "What were you needing back then?" or "What do you wish I understood about you?" You can also try writing a letter—from them to you—and allowing their voice to come through without judgment. Looking at an old photo of yourself can be powerful too. Notice the expression in your eyes.

What were you holding back? What were you proud of? What were you protecting? Sometimes, even making a playlist of songs you loved at that age can open a portal to a deeper connection. If you feel ready, speak to them in the mirror and say the words they needed to hear: "You didn't deserve that" or "You were doing your best" or, simply, "I love you." There's no right way to connect—only honest ways. Be curious. Be gentle. They've been waiting for you.

The mistake I made along the way was continuously beating myself up. Looking back, I realize I rarely let things just *be*. I was constantly analyzing my choices, especially the ones that didn't lead to immediate results. For example, I'd sign up for a new class or try a different healing practice, and if I didn't feel better right away, I'd spiral. I'd convince myself I was doing it wrong—or, worse, that there was something fundamentally wrong with me. I had no patience for the process or the messiness of real growth. Looking back, I can see how much energy I wasted fighting myself instead of just allowing myself to be human. I didn't yet know how to offer myself the same compassion I so easily gave to others. If I had been practicing that kind of self-kindness earlier on, I might have moved forward with more ease. But, as I see now, that lesson, too, was part of the path.

My shadow self is an interesting creature. There is nothing she would like more than to inflict pain on those people I love the most, not wanting me to suffer alone. *If I'm going down, you're going down with me*—I battled with this part of me for a long time. She liked to sit my family down and describe every single bad thing that had been done to me in gut-wrenching detail.

No one needed to criticize me or put me down—I did a good enough job of that all by myself. Every time I slipped up, made a mistake, or didn't heal fast enough, I'd go straight for the jugular. But you can't heal what you won't face, and for me, that meant finally calling myself out and learning a new way to be with myself.

I noticed how I'd talk to myself in ways I'd never speak to another person, punishing myself for not being further along, for having feelings, for not being "better" yet. The truth is, the voice in my head was often harsher and more relentless than anyone from my past. I had become my own judge, jury, and executioner, replaying the same old patterns of blame and shame that I was supposed to be healing from. It's one of the hardest things to admit: that sometimes the person hurting you the most is yourself. If there's one thing I've noticed about myself on this journey, it's my ability to take on the role of my own abuser.

Throughout my life—and even throughout the writing of this book—my inner teenager would pop out of the woodwork to remind me in detail of the abuse I endured. My whole life prior to my healing journey, I lived on an emotional rollercoaster, with spurts of anger that were followed by intense crying spells, instances that often took place without forewarning.

In the summer of 2013, I went out to breakfast at a local diner in my hometown after a night of drinking with my friends. We sat down and I looked at the menu, deciding I wanted a pot roast—a strange thing to order at breakfast, but I was seriously hungover. When I told the waitress what I wanted, she politely explained that they didn't have pot roast right now. The next thing I knew, I was losing my shit, shaking and yelling as my friends looked at me like I was insane.

Unable to calm down, I stormed out of the restaurant and into the parking lot, hyperventilating as I called my dad and said he needed to pick me up immediately. He drove over, hugged me, and told me everything was fine—it was just pot roast. Once I finally settled down, I felt immense shame for how I had acted.

At this time in my life, I had no idea what was going on with myself. I didn't understand triggers or trauma. I had never even heard of these words. I never even stopped to think about why I reacted the way I did. I blamed anxiety on a night of drinking. My inability to regulate my emotions, my impulsivity, and my lack of understanding how to process—these things had always just felt like "me."

But, once I discovered my past and started healing, I was able to see how all my triggers were playing out scenes from my past in present moments. I came to think back on this moment and how I had acted. Our triggers are your teachers. Had I understood that the things that trigger me were something inside being reflected back at me, I probably would have dug a little deeper. But they don't teach us that at school! We're too busy with algebra to learn about how our bodies and the universe work.

Along with these understandings came a lot of grief because remembering trauma comes with a deep sense of loss of yourself. Another thing no one teaches you is how to deal with grief, especially of something so intangible and unexplainable. I completely lost who I thought I was, like I was watching a part of me die that I would never have wished existed in the first place. Losing a part of you that you unconsciously built an entire life around—even if you don't like that part—changes you in ways you cannot foresee. It's like being given a bowl of soup after ordering a smoothie and being told that the menu has transformed since you placed your order. It's confusing, but you're hungry, so you eat it anyway.

There are many levels to this grief. It's not just grieving the person you had been; it's also grieving the person you thought you would become, the life you imagined you'd live before the memories resurfaced and the dreams you had built from that place of unknowing. It's a kind of mourning that's hard to explain because it's not always about what happened, but what *didn't*—the safety you didn't have, the support you didn't get, the version of yourself you can't be now that things are so different, the childhood you now realize you were robbed of because you were hypervigilant.

The way you view the world completely changes. You start to realize how disconnected you've been from your own body and the ways you punish yourself because of that. All the choices you made don't feel like they were yours. It's like looking back and watching someone else's life in your own body.

As I listened to my loneliness, I saw that I was overwhelmed by the grief in my body. It caused me to dissociate even more from my pain, and I did not want to let myself go there again. So, as I learned to let it come up as it presented itself, I noticed that the sadness still came, but it no longer took over my life. I was able to coexist with it. Our feelings are meant to be felt, not kept inside.

My adult self knew that my outbursts weren't necessary

to get my point across, but that didn't stop me from allowing those parts of me to speak up and be heard by the appropriate people. As I grew in age and spirituality, it became crystal clear to me that feeling these feelings was an immensely important part of my journey and that it helped so many other people too, whether they told me or not. For abuse victims, it's easy to feel lost, alone, and overwhelmed by grief. But reading even one person's story can give a hint of needed relief. This book is meant to be something you can turn to in the moments of grief, knowing you are not alone and that there is someone with a similar story who found her way to the other side. In the back of this book, you can find a list of resources that I found helpful along my journey.

As I explored these feelings, I found a lot of information that helped me understand myself. I'll never forget when I was reading about how children who experience sexual abuse or neglect experience profound effects in their prefrontal cortices, the part of the brain responsible for executive functions such as decision-making, impulse control, and emotional regulation. The trauma and stress associated with abuse may disrupt the development and functioning of this crucial brain region, potentially leading to difficulties in emotional regulation, impulse control, and cognitive processing later in life. Learning this, I thought yet again about being in that diner, as my dysregulated prefrontal cortex and I lost our shit about the pot roast.

Anger is very interesting because it's an emotion that everyone is familiar with and something we're actually encouraged to feel. Society considers it reasonable to feel outraged at the things that happen in our world; we're even looked down upon if we feel indifferent. When it comes to trauma and repressed anger from trauma, though, it's a different ball game. It's not just anger that comes up—it's complete and utter rage that lives inside of you, wanting to be released.

For much of my life, I had no control over my triggers or anger whenever they came up. I acted so extreme, only to hurt myself and anyone who was in my path. When I think of trauma and anger, my mind presents images of bombs, explosions, guns—literal war. This can be extremely overwhelming and dysregulating to be felt all at once by the nervous system. But we have to let ourselves feel it; otherwise, it will show up in other areas of life in other explosions.

At a young age, I had learned to lock my anger in a cage and let it out during sports. I would find myself on the soccer field, hip-checking girls or tackling the goalie (just because I could) or kicking the ball as hard as I could to channel my rage. Releasing anger in this way is often followed by a rush of shame. There are far healthier ways to release these feelings, especially since they are in your body.

The more you intentionally release the feeling of anger, the less potently it will show up. It becomes bearable, rational, and not something to fear. You have to feel it to move through it. Here are some things that have worked for me:

foot stomping
deep sighs
boxing
going for a walk
working out/lifting weights
screaming into or punching a pillow

screaming·outside
sweating it out in the sauna
journaling out your angry thoughts and ripping them
    up or burning them
scribbling furiously

Many books I read about healing from child sexual abuse bring up the topic of shame. The fact that survivors are ashamed of what happened to them was something that took me time to understand. I hadn't realized that those bodily sensations that made me so uncomfortable in my own skin until I wanted to crawl right out of my body and never return were feelings of shame for having "allowed" someone to touch me inappropriately. As a rational adult, I knew I hadn't been to blame for any of it, but that didn't make the shame disappear.

It took me a while to discover that being "self-conscious" was just another way of being ashamed of myself. This continuously manifested in my life through the way I viewed my own body. I was taking the unprocessed shame from my childhood and putting it back on myself as a form of control. I was obsessed with how my stomach looked and would go above and beyond to attain a flat stomach. Now, I see this makes perfect sense: Our stomach is where the solar plexus is, the part of the body that holds our personal power. As someone whose personal power was taken away at a young age, it made perfect sense that I wanted to go to great lengths to get it back. Interestingly enough, when I did physically attain a "perfectly" flat stomach, I still felt uncomfortable in my skin and full of shame.

In my body, shame is accompanied by the feeling of not

being enough: good enough, skinny enough, smart enough—you name it. Just as I had done with my sadness, I started healing my relationship with shame by feeling these feelings and making friends with them. The first step was writing down and affirming, "I love my body; it is perfect for me," over and over again. At first, I rolled my eyes and didn't believe the words, but over time, my desire to feel better overrode my ego's need to shame myself. Once I began to have a slightly better relationship with my body, I came to the realization that I didn't actually hate my body—I hated what had happened to it. Who wouldn't feel that way?

As trauma survivors, all of our feelings are valid. Do they make sense to others? Maybe not, but, my *god*, they are real to us. I hope that you, as the reader, can know that what happened to you is not your fault. The shame you feel is not yours to carry, but it is yours to transmute. You can work through it little by little. Over time, it won't feel as powerful.

Shame's partner, guilt, is another feeling that can arise unwarranted and without any notice. These feelings often make no sense when they arise. They are feelings the abuser should be feeling, not the victim. When we carry unneeded guilt, we tend to think everything is our fault, apologizing for everything and saying sorry for things we didn't even do.

When the Patriots were losing to the Falcons at the 2017 Super Bowl, I remember anxiously pacing around my house and apologizing to my family, as if the outcome were somehow my fault. I even went upstairs to the attic and cried because I was so overwhelmed by the feeling. Thank God they made a miracle comeback—who knows how I would have reacted otherwise? My emotions often didn't correspond to the present situation. Times like these are signs that there may be some repressed guilt within that is not ours to carry.

Sometimes, it's easier to blame ourselves for things that happen because it gives us a false sense of control over a situation that has us continually asking "why" something happened. Abuse is so out of our control, leaving us open, raw, and vulnerable when we are in need of safety. It is much easier for our minds to try to explain why something happened, but some things just don't have an explanation. Bad shit happens, and it is what it is.

Knowing this now, I actively practice questioning guilt when it shows up for me. I ask myself things like, "Is this true? Is this mine to carry? What is truer than the feeling I am feeling?" I also have a very active self-forgiveness protocol. Even when I know things are not my fault, I can forgive myself for having allowed myself to be in a given situation in the first place. The ho'oponopono mantra practice became a life-changing tool when feelings of guilt arose from within me.

Something significant the DBT program taught me was that anxiety is not an emotion. Hearing that something I'd been claiming to have for so long wasn't real blew my mind. At first, I couldn't wrap my mind around it, but then it finally clicked. I began to slowly peel back the layers of what had been going on in my internal world. When I experienced the sensations I had identified as anxiety, I started asking my body what I was feeling. After some time, I came to the conclusion that the "anxiety" I had been experiencing was really just fear and shame, usually about something in the future.

Once I started acknowledging my true emotions, the anxiety started to let up because identifying an emotion takes away its power over you. My trick became to notice the feeling, step back, and then tell myself that fear and shame could not rule my life. I got to choose how I wanted to feel.

Because of my history with anxiety, fear felt all too familiar, so much so that it became apparent that my body was addicted to the chemicals it released in my brain and body. Fear is sneaky and not always easy to catch. It is what saves us from being eaten by a lion, but it is not so great when it causes certain foods to send us into panic mode. Sometimes our fears aren't even ours; they are beliefs we took on from our parents or society that we accept as "just the way it is." Regardless of where our fears originated, we also have to feel them to release them.

I started to notice that the seemingly random fears I had experienced in my life were not so random after all. Once I did, I knew I needed to prove to myself that I was the one in control here. Everything in my life seemed so out of my control for so long, and it was an important part of my journey to establish some sense of control over things—but in a healthier manner. I needed to work through these feelings.

So I began doing what any extremely determined, type-A, Leo, control-freak personality would do: I took a look at each fear and said, "Fuck you, I'm doing it anyway!" Afraid of going into the basement alone? No problem—I'm there! Scared of swimming? No issues here; I'll teach myself how to swim! One by one, I began checking off these surface-level things that had been sending fear throughout my system, giving myself "corrective experiences" around the things that caused me discomfort. I felt the fear and did it anyway, and the more I did, the less afraid I felt. It brought me back to equilibrium.

Fear is often accompanied by convincing yet highly

irrational thoughts on top of trembling body sensations. Your fears know exactly how to speak to you because they are based on old stories that are unique to you. The things we have experienced in our lives, whether "good" or "bad," shape the way we feel in the present moment. Looking back, it's clear that the Universe tried to show me what had happened to me as a child through my reactions to certain situations, which were extreme beyond rationalizing. But it would be a long time before I realized that.

As horrific as my childhood trauma was, there were times it literally saved me. During the Boston Marathon bombing in 2013, I was working a promo job near the finish line. That morning, I was hit with a panic attack for "no reason." Later, when the first bomb went off, I felt it in my body before my brain could process it. I told my friend we needed to run, and seconds later, the second bomb went off where we'd just been standing. My hypervigilance—born from trauma—kept us alive.

Our triggers are our teachers. I didn't understand that then, but I see it now. We're not taught to listen to our bodies or question why certain things set us off. But, sometimes, those reactions are the reason we survive. I've learned to find gratitude for the instincts my trauma gave me. If I had ignored them, I might not be here. Life is unpredictable, painful, and miraculous all at once. Even when things don't make sense, you're always being guided to where you need to be.

Fear, anxiety, worry, and doubt are things most of us live with every day as the body's way of telling us we are in danger. What we rarely talk about is how quickly these feelings become the norm, shaping every one of our decisions, reactions, and interactions, whether we see them or not. For many of us, our subconscious programming feels so "normal" to our systems that we continue on with our lives, not realizing the deeper meaning and stories that dictate our actions.

When we're processing trauma, we may know that we "should" feel a certain way or "don't have to" feel another way, but those feelings don't always match with what we actually experience. It's best not to judge ourselves for these feelings but to let them pass through us like little visitors. If we don't, we only perpetuate them. The body is always talking to us, and it may not be making any sense, but it knows what it's doing. The more we can learn to trust the meat suit we're living in, the better we start feeling. It's a deeply personal experience, and each step is different for everyone; no one can tell us exactly how it's done, but we can all learn from each other and try things to see if they work for us.

We are not the things that happen to us; we are who we decide to be and act. Looking back, I can see that my shifts happened not all at once, but through tiny, quiet choices. Starting to ask why instead of blaming myself. Resisting the urge to try to fix myself and instead just listening. Getting curious and learning how to pause instead of spiral, how to respond instead of react. I didn't have to become someone else to heal; I just had to come back to who I had been before the world taught me to leave myself.

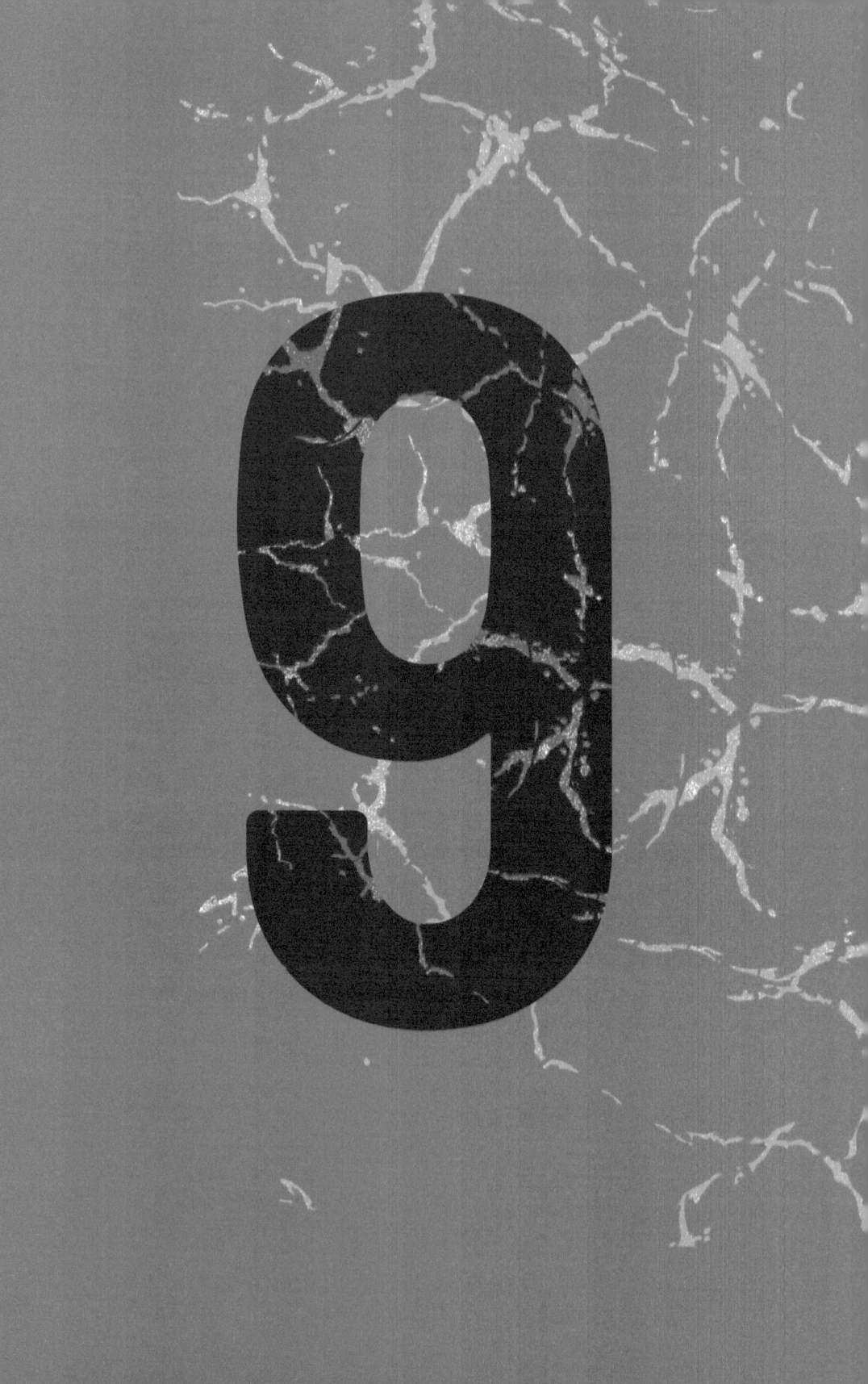

CALLING IN THE CHAOS

When others abuse their power over us, it's often not from a conscious place. When people hurt, they revert back to their own patterning from childhood—this goes for both victim and perpetrator. When we haven't yet worked through the patterns and traumas we've carried our entire lives, it's no surprise that we end up in situations that require us to pull ourselves out of them—by making different choices than those we made in the past.

So it made sense that I consistently seemed to manifest into my life people who had the ability to control me. At the time, I didn't have the tools to name it, but deep down, something always felt off with these people. Then, the more I healed, the more clearly I could see instances of manipulation for what they were. And still, I believe the Universe has a way of working everything out—especially when you choose to live in your truth. Even the people who try to use you can end up being catalysts for your awakening.

As soon as I left what I would call the "predator versus prey" energy with Cassie, things started to magically shift for me in a way I was almost not ready to receive. I was still in survival mode, on high alert as I dealt with my childhood wounding. Even though all the corrective experiences in the world were happening for me, I still had a lot of my own blocks to work through.

Really, I had one thing and one thing only on my mind: How the fuck am I going to survive? I was in deep survival and scarcity mode, running around like a chicken with its head cut off, and the number-one focus was on my finances because, face it, in this world, you need money to survive. I had not learned about the energetics of money or anything of the sort yet.

I had been connecting with a man named Josh for many months, a construction worker in his late thirties who loved nature and was introspective. He had been following me prior to my relocation to LA, and we had connected over a business endeavor I had joined at the time. Once I lived in LA, Josh and I would go for walks, and we connected deeply as friends.

On one of our walks, he said he felt God had told him he was meant to help me, just as I had helped him believe in God again after many years in the dark. I had told him about an apartment I'd found in my dream location, with two younger girls in Marina Del Rey, about a mile from where I had been before, and Josh agreed to pay my rent so I could get on my feet, not expecting anything in return. It was one of the kindest things anyone had ever done for me, and I am forever grateful, but I was far from being energetically in a place to receive this amount of help from anyone—never mind a man. I had always operated from a belief that I needed to work hard to make money, and my deepest wound was of needing to do something I didn't want to do in order to receive money. I was still running the belief that receiving money from someone would put me in danger or force me to do something bad in exchange.

Because of these beliefs around money and my inability to willingly receive at this point in my life, I had to make some hard decisions. I was desperate to stay in LA and find some stability, and I felt that if I were to tell anyone about what happened with Cassie, I would have to go back to Waltham, which was the last thing I wanted for myself. Honestly, it felt easier to stay in California, confused and suffering, than to go back and admit I'd failed. The first kind of pain was familiar; it was a pattern I'd lived in for years and one that many trauma survivors get stuck in.

I felt immense shame about the situation I got myself into since moving, and I was rarely in contact with anyone from home as a result. I felt it was best just to keep my distance rather than face the truth and the feelings of others. Was that the healthiest choice? Maybe not. But, at the time, it was what I believed I needed. Just like I struggled with receiving money, I also had blocks around receiving support. I often felt that if someone offered their opinion, I had to honor it—even if it meant betraying myself. So, instead, I shut it all out. I wasn't open to hearing anyone's opinion because I didn't yet know how to hold my truth and stay open at the same time. But the truth is, sometimes the people who love us see us more clearly than we do when we're caught in the thick of emotional chaos.

The relationship with Josh triggered me beyond belief— not because of anything he was doing, but because of all the unprocessed shit in my own subconscious mind that I hadn't dealt with. Down to his job and the car he drove, I was reminded of my abusers. He was like a perfectly packaged specimen sent from the Universe to help me work through the triggers I felt toward my uncle, but I did not have the tools or knowledge at the time to work through them.

God bless this patient man for being on the other end of this. We continued to text and talk on the phone a lot, but I had a very hard time being with him in person. The relationship invoked inside of me so many different emotions that I hadn't understood how to work with yet. Even though he had genuine intentions for me, I was very uncomfortable. Whenever I allowed myself to get too close, I would shut down and pull away.

There were several reasons for this push/pull energy. I was extremely vulnerable with this person, sharing my trauma, feelings, and truth, and I liked him as a person and appreciated everything he was doing for me. But I still felt unable to fully let go and receive, like I had this lingering energy inside that was telling me I owed him something, even as my higher mind said I had nothing to give in return.

On top of that, I wondered if I would ever be able to trust a man again after what I had been through. Even at the age of twenty-seven, it seemed nearly impossible to me. I was learning to trust the Universe, but I didn't trust myself, so I was unable to trust anyone. My past was still shaping the majority of my thoughts, which meant it was also shaping my reality.

Uncle Jeremy often gave me money after abusing me as a way of keeping me from telling anyone what had happened. He would physically shove it in my mouth, which made me viscerally ill to think about in retrospect. He had an obsession with money and material things, and I often had outbursts, claiming I wanted to take everything from him because all he cared about was money. I grew to hate money and was afraid to spend it. I also formed a deep subconscious belief that I was not worthy of money.

I had never been in a situation before where someone had offered so much more than I could give them, and it didn't feel right. Josh's financial support subconsciously made me feel like he had some sort of control over me, which activated my financial trauma on a deep level. It was a perfect storm. But I knew that my main focus needed to be on myself: my healing, growth, and expansion. So, even with all my skepticism, I took that same "fuck fear" attitude that had gotten me this far, and I did it anyway. I told myself that sometimes we have to do things we thought we never would in order to get to places we thought we'd never go.

Trauma and energy are tricky in the way that two things can be true at the same time. Even if something wasn't actually true in the present or for another person, it *felt* true to me. My nervous system was still responding to old experiences, not current ones. I could be safe now and still feel unsafe. Someone could have good intentions, and I could still feel triggered.

The meaning we give to these experiences and how we allow them to play out is what ultimately shapes our path forward. I was operating from a place of guilt and shame at this time, so that's exactly what I was creating. All Josh wanted was to be friends, but in the end, I felt so ashamed about him "taking care" of me that I couldn't even do that. Eventually, we cut ties, as it was no longer healthy for either of us.

Unable to receive his help, I went back to worrying about how I was going to make enough money to eat. Wanting to retain control however I could, I returned to another old pattern I had yet to break free from. I took my crazy workout regime, basically the only thing that helped me feel good, to the next level. Soon, I was working out at least twice a day, either at the gym or at yoga classes, and my hyper-focus on my body was intense.

I didn't know what to believe in anymore, so I spent the majority of my time immersing myself in knowledge about spirituality and manifestation. I read books, listened to podcasts, and watched videos, learning everything and anything about how to get myself out of this financial situation. I filled up notebook after notebook with affirmations, numerology codes, and future scripting, trying to make my way through the world. At this point, I was also smoking a lot of weed and constantly living in my mind. I had not worked through any of my "blockages" or the trauma stored in my body, and although these techniques seemed to be working for me, they were not aligned with my highest good.

So I did what anyone would do—I hit Craigslist. This landed me several different TV shows, modeling gigs, and other stuff I'm not very proud of. It's not that any of them were particularly bad; it's just that I was accepting way less than I knew I deserved. Had I not, first of all, been on drugs and, second of all, known how to work with my own unique energy and trust myself, I wouldn't have done some of these gigs. After all, guilt, shame, and Adderall can cause you to make decisions you might not have thought you would.

I'm grateful for these experiences because they are things I can say I did, but this was still me being stuck in my old pattern of doing things for money that didn't feel good for me, all stemming back to the original childhood wound. That kind of wound will sneak in and run your life until you're fully conscious of it.

Now, it may sound like a positive thing to work so hard for the sake of making money and surviving, but let me tell you something about energy. When you are coming from a place of lack, carrying a lot of guilt and shame from trauma that wants to release from your body, you might find yourself in some crazy situations. Entrenched in all of this and so focused on survival energy, I refused to see how I *was* supported. I was so focused on what I didn't have, constantly looking for side gigs or ways to make money, that I couldn't see that I did have enough.

The time came when I knew I had to figure out some sort of stable job on top of all the side gigs I was doing. I loved having the days to myself and didn't go out at night anyway, so I decided that waitressing or bartending would be a good fit for me. A friend of a friend owned a Santa Monica bar called The Britannia, a cross between a British pub and a hub for people to come watch the Philadelphia Eagles football games. I went for an interview and was immediately hired.

Once I started working there, I felt a significant change in my energy. I was spending a lot of time with friends and having healthy social experiences. A lot of the people I had met had been in similar situations to mine and were also starting over, working through trauma, and trying to find their way in this new territory of Los Angeles. Finding others to connect with helped me realize I wasn't alone and gave me support and perspective. It reminded me that healing didn't have to be a solo experience, and being around people who understood my struggles made the process feel less isolating and more possible.

I was also trying to date again. My dating life had been messy since my awakening, but despite the shit I'd gone through with my boss boyfriend, I promised myself that I wouldn't allow that to have power over me (like my childhood trauma). I believed there were good men out there, and I would continue in my search for love.

Between loving my new apartment, going to the beach every day, hanging out with my friends, and finally having some sort of stable work, I began to see a drastic expansion in my manifestations. Prior to this, my written manifestations and affirmations didn't seem to come true. But, as soon as I felt settled in this space in my life, things started flying—within hours and even minutes at times. I would set an intention, think of something in particular, and *boom*, it would be there. I was feeling like the witchiest witch.

One night, while I was doing some journaling and manifestation, I decided to play around with the idea of becoming an actress. I wrote down that I was an actress on a TV show, and then I just kind of let it go. I had always thought about being an actress, but it felt more like a fantasy that I was excited about than something I had never really put much effort into.

The next day, I received a message from a woman named Marla about a pair of ripped jeans I had posted on Facebook Marketplace. I had done lots of online selling and thought nothing of it as I met the buyer outside my place. Then, she asked if I wanted to be on a TV show. Marla's daughter was an actress, she explained, and they were putting together a show that she thought I would be perfect for. She told me to think about it and get back to her soon. It would be starting next week with a photoshoot in Arizona and a table read for the pilot. I thanked her and walked away in shock.

What in the world was happening to me? How was everything I was writing down and visualizing actually happening? Did I just figure out the key to life? What I learned was this: Manifestation doesn't happen from desperation—it happens from alignment. I had spent so long trying to call things in from a place of lack, or urgency, or needing proof. Once I finally felt grounded—safe in my space, supported in my work, surrounded by joy—things began to flow effortlessly.

The energy had shifted because *I* had shifted. I wasn't gripping anymore. I wasn't trying to force the outcome. I was living in the vibration of trust, and the Universe was responding in real time. That exchange wasn't just a "sign"; it was a reflection. A wink from the divine. Looking back now, it's wild to me how fast I can manifest when I have even a glimpse of good feelings and have left survival mode. A reminder that when you're anchored in your truth and open to receiving, life will meet you in the most magical, unexpected ways.

I've come to learn since that money is energy. At its core, it's a neutral force that flows where there's alignment, intention, and belief. Our relationship with money often reflects our relationship with self-worth, safety, and receiving. If we carry unhealed stories around scarcity, shame, or not feeling "enough," it can block the flow. But when we start to shift our energy by honoring our value, releasing fear, and creating from a place of purpose, we begin to magnetize money instead of chasing it. Using the energetics of money means working not just with strategy but with vibration: tending to your mindset, your nervous system, and your beliefs so you can hold and grow what flows in. Money isn't just a resource; it's a mirror. And when you heal the reflection, you change what's attracted to you.

I was starting to feel powerful as hell, but that didn't mean I wasn't still traumatized as hell. My ability to discern wasn't as crystal clear as I thought, but my ability to trust was climbing its way up there. The next day, I texted the woman and told her I was in. I had no idea what I was doing, and this was a whole new world to me, but I felt like I could trust her. Almost by magic, I seemed to have called her in through my manifestations. I was elated. Little did I know that I was about to set myself up for yet another in a series of lessons.

LOSING MY MIND, FINDING MY SOUL

It felt like things in my life were coming together. I was working, and my spare time was spent working out at Gold's Gym, rollerblading at the beach, going to movie premieres, networking, and acting in feature films. I got a publicist and a manager, and I even started dating someone! Physically, he was not my type, and he was ten years older, but his intellect, humor, and work-obsessed behavior fed my pattern of attracting emotionally unavailable men who had no time for me. We were going on fun dates and spending time together, and it seemed like everything was looking up—finally. I thought my life was about to begin.

Over the next six months, I became extremely close with Marla and her thirteen-year-old daughter, who had been in the entertainment world since she was a young child and had been taken advantage of by older men on a few occasions. Marla had read my posts online and could deeply relate to my trauma because of this. I felt very connected to her, knowing their family had experienced similar things on a large scale—from relatives as well as within the realm of Hollywood, where her father was very involved in the business.

We connected over not only the show and other acting opportunities but also our deep desire to attain justice and revenge for abuse victims. I say this because it's important to know where our energy was coming from and where it was going. If you're coming from a place of love, you'll get love back. If you're coming from a place of revenge, well …

It's important to remember that, at this time, I was still on all of those medications the doctor had prescribed to me. I want to make it clear that I am not demonizing medication, but there does come a point in one's journey when we have to pay back the emotional loan we take out while we are on it. I was numbed out, unable to *feel* what was going on around me, and just following whatever I *thought* was right. But I continued trying my best to tuck away my mountain of lingering anxiety, chalking it up to the fact that I was just someone who was traumatized.

A lot of my actions were rooted in a place of revenge. I wanted to show my abusers that they couldn't control me and that I would "show them." Then, they'd have to look at how amazing I was doing, despite what they had done. This attitude fueled me and pushed me to continue into places (the entertainment industry) that I found to be—quite literally—insane.

Marla and I would spend hours on the phone talking about helping prevent children from being harmed by adults, and our relationship made me feel like I was actually living out my purpose. Simultaneously, she brought me into the world of television and film. I was meeting a ton of people, going to premieres, and networking with people for potential roles in different projects. I was new to this world, and she often told me exactly what to say or do, and I would blindly listen. There is a time and a place for blind faith, like when you're waiting for your manifestations to come to fruition, but we shouldn't necessarily listen to everything others tell us without question.

I noticed Marla would spin fake stories about my history in the acting world. As someone who doesn't lie and tends only to speak the blunt truth, I couldn't help but feel uncomfortable when she did this. But I went along with it because I was told it was the only way I could get work. I was young, naive, traumatized, and my eyes were on the prize: proving myself.

I started signing contracts with my new manager for different projects that were set to start filming in a few months. This had me elated, so excited that my acting career was taking steps in the right direction. I was attending industry parties and premieres, events where I had to put on my "character" and become Gabriella the actress. When I first started going to these events, everything was fine, but then a switch flipped. Things started to get weird.

At a horror film premiere on Halloween, I was on the dance floor with Marla's daughter when I noticed an old man grabbing her ass. I immediately freaked out and started screaming at him, telling him not to touch her and that she was a child. She and her mom thanked me for sticking up for her, but the next day, I received an enraging message from the publicist Marla had connected me with.

"Gabriella needs to control herself," it read. "She made people feel really uncomfortable last night."

This sent me to a new level of anger I hadn't known

existed. How could I be getting in trouble for sticking up for a child being touched? Feeling like I had to be a bystander to the same type of abuse I had experienced as a kid was deeply triggering.

I was also discouraged by industry people from "telling my story," so I began to shy away from sharing what I had been so open about for the previous three years. I had been told this was a way to protect me, but it also didn't feel in alignment with my vision.

So I blindly handed over my power (again), allowing myself to be told when and what to post online. I was accepting of this, as there seemed to be a future "prize" or "reward" promised for my obedience. But was it me acting out a childhood pattern of "be the good girl, keep your mouth shut, and you won't get hurt"? Absolutely. Was I able to see this at the time? Absolutely not. Did the Universe blow up my world to show me this? Yes. When you are not in alignment, the Universe will take drastic measures to make sure you get to where you need to be.

Another few weeks went by, and we were invited to a big award event—people flying in from all over the country, big names, big energy. I was excited. I was told there could be real opportunity waiting for me there. But then everything unraveled.

One thing led to another and I found out this young actress's mom had fabricated an elaborate story about her husband being sick. Turns out, it was drugs. She didn't show up to the event. I ended up meeting her at the hospital later that night. She looked me in the eye and told me this was the end of the road for her— but that I should keep going.

I said my goodbyes. I never heard from her again.

She was yet another example of someone I allowed to have power over me—someone I thought held the keys to my future. But this time, they let me go. And maybe that was the gift. I walked away disturbed by what I had seen in the entertainment industry. Something in me knew if I was going to keep walking this path, it would have to be on my own terms. The illusion had cracked. And something in me had started to wake up.

Shortly after, a close friend I hadn't seen in a while invited me over and asked me if I had any interest in moving into a penthouse with her. She had been looking at places and found one she loved but needed a roommate. It was a beautiful, two-story apartment in the heart of West Hollywood, a place where several celebrities lived at the beginning of their careers. I loved the sound of the apartment—spacious, with big windows and a balcony—and even though the rent was significantly higher than I was currently paying, I rested assured knowing I had a job at the restaurant, and would find a way to make it work, like I always did. With all the magic I was seeing happening around me, I had deep faith that I could trust where this was pushing me. Everything else seemed to be working out, so why wouldn't this?

The next day, my friend and I went out for lunch and a walk, and I received a text message from one of the managers at my work. "Thank you so much for all your hard work," it read. "We are no longer in need of your services, as the high season has come to an end." I was in shock. Did I just get laid off (via text!) the day after I had committed to moving into a new apartment? Yes, I sure did. I hadn't even had a clue I was a "seasonal employee."

It sent me into an immediate fight-or-flight response. What was I supposed to do now? I freaked out for a bit, then came to my senses and realized I could get another waitressing job that was closer to the new apartment anyway. So I sent out multiple applications, went to some interviews, and ended up getting a job at the famous Formosa Cafe. One of my friends from Instagram was the manager there, and he gladly hired me. Job secured, so we're good, right? You'll see.

As my new roommate and I grew closer, we got into discussions about medication. She expressed some concerns for me, specifically regarding Adderall. I had been blindly popping whatever the doctors gave me for nine years by then, without thinking much more about it. But I trusted her, and we had a mutually loving friendship. I had shared my deep, dark truth with her and been met with open arms. So, with her support, I decided I would taper off all the medications. What were they really doing for me, anyway? I was still having flashbacks, and I had learned how to deal with them. I figured, why the hell not?

Although this was probably the best thing I would ever do for myself, I don't recommend doing it the way I did. If you are on medication and want to get off, do it with the assistance of your medical provider. By the time the medications left my system, not only could I feel for the first time, but all the parts of me that I had suppressed for so long started coming to the surface, showing themselves to anyone and everyone around me. I was out of control, and no one knew what to do with me.

Here's the thing: It's one thing to talk about dissociation, but not even being able to recognize you're dissociating into completely different versions of yourself—without any control of your mind—is an entirely different ball game. I will never forget the morning I woke up and looked around my room (where I had been living for two months) and had no idea where I was or who my roommate was. That is when I realized that, all this time I thought I had been healing, I was really just being controlled by my medicine.

That moment marked a turning point. When I shifted from just coping with what I'd experienced to actually *processing* it, the unraveling was brutal—especially once I started realizing the things I'd done while medicated that I wouldn't have chosen in a clearer state. I got to learn self-reconciliation when dealing with thoughts about being a "bad" person for the choices I made. That added a whole new layer of shame I had to sit with because there was no one to blame but myself. But it also meant there was no one to forgive but myself, and when I gave myself that forgiveness, it set me free.

Long story short, coming off medication opened up a whole new world for me. I could suddenly feel my emotions and those of others around me. This was exciting, scary, and infuriating, all at the same time. I didn't know what to do with any of it, which only caused me to enter an even deeper state of hypervigilance. I overanalyzed everything and perceived everything as a threat, disturbed by intrusive thoughts that everyone around me was a pedophile or wanted to hurt me. I could barely sleep, so I was exhausted and wired at the same time. I felt like I had no control over myself and asked myself who I was every day because I genuinely did not know anymore. I was left with the mess of things I had created while I was medicated.

I had lived my life trying to keep myself safe, and that is all my body knew. Now, just walking near someone, I could feel their emotions, allowing them to trigger whatever was unprocessed inside of me. At the drop of a hat or a shift in someone's energy, I could go from being elated to crying hysterically. This did not serve me, as it left me energetically open and without any sense of self.

The openness left me vulnerable in other ways too. I was still learning how to hold boundaries, especially in spiritual spaces where it *felt* like everyone had good intentions. That's when I met a "shaman," who claimed she was helping me by "shamanically unlocking" all of my unprocessed parts. At first, I believed her. I *wanted* to believe her. But she soon began asking me to drive her around, help her with her brand, and, eventually, pay her for the "healing" work she had initiated. In hindsight, this was a softer replay of the dynamic I'd experienced with both Cassie and Marla.

Looking back, I can see I was still in a phase where I equated spiritual signs with spiritual truth and yet learned that signs without discernment can still lead to manipulation. But the experience taught me something invaluable: Being open-hearted doesn't mean being wide open to everyone. Discernment isn't judgment; it's self-trust.

As I got away from the medications, I began to develop a deep inner rage toward myself and the medical system that had encouraged me to take them. I started to question everything I had ever learned from doctors, swaying from complete trust in them to total distrust. I went to the gynecologist to get my IUD removed and found out it had been causing me pain and body flashbacks as a reminder to my body of what had happened to me as a child. The realization gave me yet another reason to turn my back on the medical community.

But if I couldn't trust doctors to help me, who *could* I trust? I reached a point where I refused to take any pill for anything. I wouldn't touch ibuprofen, afraid it was going to hurt me. I had swung from one end of the spectrum to the complete opposite. The girl who had once had a pill for everything was going to live life holistically.

By the beginning of 2020, I was off of everything. Now, I had a new challenge: figuring out how to get all the parts of me that had been so willingly taking over my life under control. Gabby was trying to get me to be a personal trainer. Gabbith wanted to run off to her cotton candyland and be a four-year-old. Gab was absolutely mortified, and Gabriella just wanted to go home to her family.

I continued to see my therapist, who told me I was bipolar and encouraged me to get back on medication. I assured her that I wasn't bipolar, that I had severe trauma and was dissociating, and that I wouldn't get back on medication. I even sought out additional therapy, but all I kept hearing was that I needed to go back on medication. If these people weren't going to listen to or help me, I figured I had no choice but to ride it out and find a way to help myself. So I took to my journal and turned my focus toward trying to create something for my coaching business.

I was still working at the Formosa, making decent money and starting to see that I could actually take care of myself. Despite the dissociating, my confidence was growing, and I was learning to accept and deal with the way certain parts of me took over at times. I spent a lot of time trying to "integrate" these parts and believed I could kill them off, make them go away, and just be a "normal" person. But I had no such luck, so I decided, fuck it, I'll be the dissociating girl. It is what it is, and it's fine with me as long as I have money to survive and live my life.

Then, March 2020 hit. I lost my job as the world shut down. Here we go again, I thought. During the COVID pandemic, it felt like everyone else was finally experiencing what I'd already lived through. The isolation, uncertainty, life turned upside down—none of it was new to me. If anything, I was a pro at surviving chaos by then.

There was so much happening in the world, and for the first time in a long time, I stopped obsessing over my healing. I had gotten to the point where I nitpicked everything about myself, and it wasn't helping anymore. I needed to pause. To breathe. To clear the slate. So I did. I still had flashbacks, but I was done making a project of myself. I started to accept myself as I was.

While the world was shutting down, I decided it was my time to break free. I started hiking every day, claiming space for myself and choosing freedom in a way I never had before. I made a clear decision: I wasn't going to participate in the chaos. I had already begun waking up to how much the media was shaping our perception, and I knew I didn't want to be brainwashed or controlled anymore. I wasn't putting anything up my nose, and I sure as hell wasn't letting anyone tell me what to do. I'd been controlled for too long.

PART THREE

CONNECT WITH OTHERS

THE REWARD IN THE RUINS

I found myself progressively feeling better as the days of the pandemic passed by, but the rage I felt about my childhood trauma continued to linger inside of me. Almost two years had passed since I had filed the police report, and I still hadn't heard back from the detectives. I knew they had spoken privately to both my ex-boyfriend and my parents, but there had been no movement since. I had no way of knowing whether my abusers were still hurting people, but the fear that it was possible was enough to keep me up at night. I couldn't live with the idea of turning a blind eye to the abuse I knew others might be experiencing, and I felt an overwhelming responsibility to expose my abusers. The sense of responsibility weighed on me constantly, driving me to speak up, even when it cost me.

One afternoon spent rollerblading, sitting in the sand, and journaling in Venice Beach, I heard from the guy I had met in spin class years ago, who had first encouraged me to take legal action against my abusers. He had finished school, passed the bar, and was now working at a law firm. He felt now would be a good time for me to follow through with the lawsuit I had set out to pursue years ago.

By now, it was the end of 2020, and my life was shifting and changing once again. Christmas was quickly approaching, and after visiting my family for the holiday, I was set to move out of the penthouse and into my own spot in Santa Monica. I had missed living by the beach and found it very helpful for my mental health. I finally felt strong enough and ready to pursue this lawsuit, and my two-week trip to the East Coast might give me the chance to get this thing done before starting a new chapter for myself. So I spent the next month putting together all the information I had gathered over the years in preparation for speaking with the lawyer. Then, I packed up my room at the penthouse and flew back to my parents' place for the first time in two years.

The return home was the first time I would be seeing my extended family and friends since getting off all of my medications. Knowing I would be there, feeling the energy of the scene of the crime, so to speak, added a whole other layer of stress to my homecoming. Equally, without the meds in my system, I was able to hear Spirit loud and clear. Now, I wasn't just the girl who remembered she was sexually abused, lost her mind, and had multiple personalities. I was also the weird spiritual girl who thought she could hear dead people. So I got home carrying the belief that everyone thought I was insane—and this was when I would finally talk to the lawyers. This trip would be a breeze.

In order to meet with the lawyers, I needed to bring a detailed transcript of the abuse. But, every time I tried to sit down and write one, I couldn't get myself to do it. Time and time again, I would try to write, with no results—just immense pain and body flashbacks that had me bedridden. I needed to find someone who would transcribe for me everything that was circulating in my head, someone I felt safe with and who could emotionally handle everything they were about to hear.

I ended up asking my friend Andria, who is like a sister to me, and she agreed. So I went to her office, lay down on her esthetician's table, and through tears, spit out everything as she typed away like a mad secretary. This was not an easy process for me. Although I had shared a lot of details with other people in my life, exposing essentially everything made me dissociate like crazy. We sometimes forget how talking about things can cause all the feelings and energy of that time to resurface. But we got the job done, and I was so grateful that she had held the space and for it to finally be over and done.

When it came time to meet with the lawyers, I was both anxious and excited. Finally, it seemed that justice was on the horizon and I was one step closer to freedom. I was first greeted by the guy from my spin class, and then I was taken to the legal team, where I provided all the details they asked for. The lawyer informed me that I needed to be aware of something: if I were to pursue legal action, the other side would very likely claim I was just trying to become famous. When I heard this, I sat there dumbfounded, confused as to why anyone would want to be famous for being sexually abused by their family members.

As we were wrapping up, they told me they would be in touch to let me know if they were going to take the case. In my mind, though, it was a done deal. Who could hear all that horrific stuff and *not* want to help me? The rest of my trip felt a little lighter, and, returning to LA, I was excited to start my new chapter. It would be my first time living alone in my own space and fully supporting myself.

On February 23, 2021, I went for my daily workout at Gold's Gym. It was leg day, and the sun was shining— perfect weather for an outdoor workout. So I went outside, surrounded by all of the influencers recording themselves, and started lifting. I was jamming out to my music and just feeling the vibes when, all of a sudden, I went to switch the weight off of the barbell on the squat rack, and two forty-five-pound plates flew off the rack and landed right on my left foot. I fell to the ground in complete shock as employees rushed over to help me up.

Me being myself, I cracked jokes the entire time, trying to distract myself from the pain as I was carried to a back room where a trainer iced my foot and insisted I go to the hospital. I complied and drove myself to the hospital, where I found out I had broken not one but two of my toes and needed surgery as soon as possible. As someone who works out for her livelihood and sanity, I was very upset and at a loss of what I would do.

Leaving the emergency room, I got a phone call from the lawyer I had met with, who regretted to inform me that they would not be taking the case. With that, I burst into tears. *Is this the worst day of my life?* I thought. There I was, living alone, paying my rent with the physical labor I could no longer do, and now hearing that I would not be getting justice after all. This could not be real. My ego was pissed.

Living truly alone and in my own space was an eye-opening experience for me. It was the first time in my life that I could directly feel my own energy, which was both amazing and frightening. Those initial months brought realization after realization about how other people's energies had been affecting me for my entire life, and how I had no conscious awareness of it. In my physical reality growing up, I was used to being in crowded spaces, sharing a home with one bathroom, thin walls, and absolutely no privacy between five people. We all had big personalities, big energy, and little to no emotional regulation. It was no surprise that I was unable to feel myself. Considering all of my trauma history, I was happy to be deaf to it all.

So there I was, back to square one. The injury stripped me of many of the tools I regularly relied on to help myself feel remotely okay. It was a big wake-up call from the Universe. As I lay on the couch for days, I contemplated how I obviously needed to find a new way to live my life. Revenge for my childhood wasn't going to work. Being abusive to my body over and over again through overexercising wasn't going to work. Those two options were finally off the table. But what was I supposed to do now? The only thing left was to let go and see what would unfold. I had done it before, albeit with a lot of anxiety, and this time I knew I couldn't do that to myself. Unable to exercise, I didn't have an outlet for my stress. I had to simply trust in the unfolding.

Within the next couple of weeks, my friend told me about a COVID rent relief program. Once I applied and was accepted, there was one issue I no longer had to worry about. *Check.* Then, an acting friend I had started dating was looking for paid streamers for a new app called Pococha. I joined the app and was paid $800 a month for a few hours of streaming a week. So I went on every day, led a meditation, and provided some helpful affirmations. *Another check*. Once again, the Universe was supplying. Everything was going to be okay.

As I continued to feel good about how things were unfolding, I reached out again to my friend's uncle, who lived in Vegas. He reiterated that ayahuasca would really help with my body flashbacks but said that if I wasn't ready, I could start by microdosing mushrooms, taking a small amount of psilocybin, and that would help fire up new brain neurons and develop new neural pathways.

This time, when he made the suggestion, I had been off medication for about a year, so I figured I might as well give it a try. A few phone calls later, I was introduced to a friend of a client who made microdoses, and I put in an order. Thus began my microdosing journey. I would take a small amount and simply go about my day. Soon, I noticed I felt happier, more present, and capable of accepting my circumstances as they were, instead of constantly harboring the past. *Check, check, check*.

While I was livestreaming a meditation one afternoon, a viewer of mine commented that she loved my Boston accent and what I was doing. I went into her stream later that day and saw that she had a similar mission and stream to mine. We both had been hired by the same company, so we exchanged numbers and started texting here and there about the gig. She was going through a tough time, and I felt connected to her in a strange way I didn't know how to describe. She lived in San Francisco at the time but was planning on moving to LA, and I felt we were meant to be friends, so I suggested we go hiking once she had moved. That's how I met my future best friend and business partner, Gina.

For the next year, my life would look pretty simple. I was neither elated nor sad, no longer experiencing the ups and downs of my past. I was just okay, and that's more than I can say for any other year I had experienced. That summer, I turned thirty.

When 2022 rolled around, I was making enough money bartending that I quit streaming. I also ended my relationship with my actor friend. We parted ways on good terms, but I gave myself some space to heal. It was so different from when I broke up with my boss boyfriend and felt so betrayed and hurt. This time, it just wasn't a match. There was no drama, just clarity. That's how I knew I was making the right choice. When I started dating again a few months later, I was going to do it differently: I was ready to manifest my partner.

There were a few different moving parts to my manifesting antics. I got super clear on what I was looking for. I would go on walks with other single girlfriends of mine, and we would talk about what we wanted in our dream partners. I knew I wanted someone who worked for himself (so he would have plenty of time for me) and wanted to provide for me. I also wanted someone who was going to understand me and the trauma I had been through.

I had previously found it challenging to try to "teach" someone else how to understand me (my trauma, body flash-backs, moods, etc.), which often led to me feeling misunderstood or unheard. Now, I can't expect people to understand others' trauma, but with the level of trauma I was carrying, feeling understood was crucial to me. My mother, too, had always told me that I needed someone strong, who understood me and could handle me—not because there was ever anything wrong with me, but just because of the magnitude of my internal and external experiences, which weren't for the faint of heart. All trauma survivors need to feel a sense of understanding and compassion for the process they go through. From now on, anything less than that would be a hard no for me.

When I shared this with others, I was often told things like, "You shouldn't limit yourself like that" or "A guy doesn't have to understand to love you." But I knew by now what I wanted in my heart. I wanted to be with someone who was open to doing this work with me, who wanted to learn and grow like I did. I knew that—somehow, somewhere—there was someone out there for me. I didn't have any evidence, but I had intuition. I was working hard on trusting myself.

I knew that no matter what, I needed to put energy into dating if I wanted to get the results I wanted. So I set the intention, let go of my attachments to what was to come, and started swiping on the dating apps. I went out on dates with people even if I wasn't extremely attracted to them, where I previously only did so when I felt intense attraction. As such, I left most dates knowing I had no interest in a further connection with the person yet feeling good about the fact that I was putting the effort and energy toward meeting the right person.

Finding a life partner was still on my radar, but I wasn't just waiting around for him. I was enjoying everything fun about dating until the right person actually showed up (and maybe that's what made it possible). There was no attachment and no projection. Just clarity, trust, and openness. The key to manifesting is letting go of the "how" something is going to come and just allowing it to show up as it's meant to. And that's exactly what happened.

At the time, I was working several different jobs, one of them as a bartender-hostess on yachts in the Marina. Not only was I making money, but I felt very connected to God while I was on the water. There was something about the way it moved—steady, unpredictable, vast—that mirrored something sacred in me. Being out there, surrounded by nothing but sky and sea, it felt like I had entered into a direct conversation with the divine. I felt completely at peace, like I had stepped out of the noise of the world and into a place where I could finally hear.

Being on the water required me to release the grip I had on needing to know, needing to predict, needing to protect myself. There was no illusion of control out there. I wasn't guaranteed safety. There was no certainty about what might come next. And yet, I trusted. I surrendered. I just had to *be*. And in that being, I felt held. Protected. Cradled by something so much bigger than me. It was the ultimate act of trust. In that trust, I found God—not as an idea, but as a felt presence. A knowing in my bones.

One day in April, I went to the bow of the boat and declared, "Okay, God. I am ready for love." I had been enjoying my hot girl summer and dating with the intention of putting out that energy, but I finally felt ready for my person to come. I had never declared it as powerfully and embodied as I did that day.

That particular day, there was a nice crew of people I had enjoyed chatting with on the boat, and I planned on exchanging Instagrams with one of the guys at the end of the charter.

When he handed me his phone, I typed in my Instagram and saw that we were both following this guy, Zack, another trauma coach who shared his own trials and tribulations along with lots of amazing healing content. We had been following each other for a year (I have no idea how I found him), and I loved what he posted. I turned to the man whose phone I was holding and said, "Oh, you know Zack!" as if I knew him personally.

Walking away from that interaction, I was caught off guard by my own behavior. Why had I acted like I knew some random guy on Instagram? Genuinely astonished, I decided to reach out to him and share how I had acted like I knew him to a complete stranger. He responded immediately, and we shared a laugh. Then, we got to chatting a little bit about trauma and dissociation, laughing together about the absurdities of this journey. He asked me if I would want to talk on Zoom some-time, and we scheduled a time to talk the next day. Little did I know, my entire life was about to change for the better.

From the very beginning, my relationship with Zack felt divinely guided—on both of our ends. This wasn't something I forced or created a fantasy around. It was delivered to me. I wasn't searching for it, and I definitely wasn't grasping for it like I had in the past. I had reached a place where I was genu-inely okay—with or without a partner. And not in a "let me say this to manifest someone" way, but in a full-bodied, grounded way. I meant it. And when you *feel* it like that, the energy you're putting out lands completely differently.

The day we scheduled our meeting, I had spent a lot of time at the beach, doing my daily grounding and manifes-tation. When we hopped on Zoom, it was like a thousand fireworks exploded as we giggled, chatted, and shared deep conversations. Even though we were complete strangers and only meeting virtually, it was a level of connection and a strong surge of energy like neither of us had ever experienced before.

Zack and I started texting and video chatting every day from that point forward. He was living in Philadelphia, and three days after our initial call, he booked a flight to come visit me later that month. He had always wanted to live in LA, and we even discussed what it would look like if he moved there within that first week of talking. We both acknowledged the absurdity of the whole situation, making jokes about whether we were love bombing each other or completely out of our minds, but our intuitions felt like they were on fire.

We deeply understood each other, both coming from a history of child sexual abuse and actively doing the work to heal and grow from it. We had the same vision in life, and without even knowing one another, we both truly felt like we had met our match. It felt like a gift from God, the answer to my prayers (and my mother's!). All of the signs were flooding in, and there was no denying that no matter what the outcome would be, there was something very special about our connection.

I spent the next few weeks preparing my apartment for Zack to arrive. I got new bedding and linens, rearranged my belongings, and cleaned like I had never cleaned before. I wanted to put my best self forward. The moment he arrived at my apartment, a second round of fireworks went off inside. We spent hours talking and really leaning into the strong feelings we were both experiencing. When he asked me to be his girlfriend, of course, I accepted. We had no idea how we were going to make the long distance work, but we knew we would figure it out. After Zack left that first visit, I knew I had found my life partner.

A week later, I received a text from my new friend, Gina, saying she had moved to Ventura and that the meditation she'd planned to attend in Malibu that day had been canceled. Excited, I insisted she come over, and within an hour, she was at my house. Just like I had sensed when we met online, we had an immediate connection. We got to talking and learned we had both been through relatively recent breakups. When she asked me what was going on with my love life, I told her she would probably think I was nuts but that I met someone online who lives across the country. She replied that I would probably think she's nuts because she met someone across the *globe*. She asked me what my new guy's name was, and I said Zack. She gasped and looked me dead in the eyes as she said her guy's name was Zac. We both got instant chills. What kind of crazy "coincidence" is that?

We proceeded from there, building our friendship by going on hikes, getting to know each other, and coming to the realization over and over again that we had more in common with our life experience than we would be able to explain in words. Everything in our lives seemed to mirror one another's, and we both felt seen, heard, and understood by each other in a way that neither of us had ever experienced before. We both shared a passion for the entertainment industry as well as a life's mission and purpose: to help others who had been abused. The profound safety and understanding we experienced together felt divinely orchestrated.

While hiking one day, we decided that we would put both of our visions together and start a company to help others.

After the hike, we went to the beach and saw two bunnies hopping across the path before us. And just like that, Bunny Bunny Productions was born, creating a platform to tell real, raw stories that help trauma survivors feel seen, heard, and understood.

Since then, Gina and I have created content, experiences, and site-specific resources for sexual-abuse survivors, breaking the silence around pain and healing and building a community rooted in truth and compassion. Our mission is to empower survivors to reclaim their voices, spark honest conversations, and support each person on their unique journey to purpose, peace, and fulfillment—reminding everyone that they are not alone.

As Gina and I grew closer, Zack and I continued to talk every day. He returned for a few more visits over the next two months, and our conversations focused on topics of our life goals, healing, and how we were both learning to become the best versions of ourselves while integrating all the old parts of us and doing the work that is required on this journey. We made space and allowed for all the parts of both of us to be seen, heard, and loved as we navigated life.

Before meeting Zack, I had been doing a lot of internal work—on my own and in solitude. But even with all that progress, I started to feel like my growth had plateaued. I was still getting triggered, still stuck in certain patterns, and something in me knew: *I've come as far as I can on my own for now.*

I needed someone who could gently mirror things back to me that I couldn't always see for myself. Being in partnership with someone who is loving, honest, and emotionally aware helped activate that new layer of my healing. I needed reflection, and that's exactly what Zack brought into my life. And while the road hasn't been perfect, it's been real. Loving. Confronting. Sacred. For the first time in a long time, I wasn't just surviving—I was growing *with* someone. Zack helped me feel supported to be myself and to trust myself, and for that I am forever grateful.

Our relationship isn't just about romance or connection—it's been a container for accelerated growth. It helped put me back on track. Not because he completed me, but because I had finally done enough inner work to meet someone from a place of wholeness. This wasn't a story that I had made up to feel safe. It was a truth I recognized the moment it arrived.

Zack also encouraged me to reconnect with my family, since over a year had passed since my last trip back home. He felt it was important for my healing process, and, now that we'd been together for a few months, I felt ready to introduce him to everyone. Rummaging through my old journals before the trip, I stumbled across an entry from 2018 where I was manifesting my future partner. In the notebook, I found a word-for-word description of Zack and our relationship—even down to his name. I literally wrote "Zack" in 2018! This freaked me out, but it also confirmed to me that manifesting was real and that this was my partner. He was even from Philadelphia—a huge Eagles fan—which felt like a full-circle moment, bringing me back to the bar where I landed my first job in LA, which always played their games.

When August rolled around, we happily went to see my family and had an amazing time. Zack fit right in, just as I had suspected he would, and he helped add another level to my sense of safety. With him there, I felt my feet were firmer on the ground, that I knew who I was and was willing to stand in my convictions, no matter what anyone else thought. It was the first time since I had moved to California that I truly enjoyed my time at home and didn't want to leave. It was with a happy heart that I flew back to LA as Zack returned to Philadelphia.

Over a span of six months, the building and neighborhood I was living in grew progressively more dangerous. We knew it was time for me to leave. Without hesitation, Zack packed up his things, got out of his lease, and flew to LA. We decided we would travel the world for a year until we figured out where we wanted to land. He was not going to save me, but he wanted to protect me.

Although things were going well in my relationship, my body continued causing me problems. I had been doing the internal work and somatic work for so long, but nothing so far was alleviating the physical symptoms I was still constantly experiencing in my body. Sudden bouts of sharp pain in my vagina continued to knock me off my feet.

The body flashbacks showed no sign of going anywhere; I had just grown used to them with time. Though they didn't make me cry or cause much distress like in previous years, they brought on an overwhelming feeling that I would never be able to leave the past. It was still haunting me from inside, even when I wasn't consciously thinking about it. And the constant sting of pain from the past was not something I wanted to bring into this next chapter of my life.

THE SHOCKING GIFT OF
SURRENDER

Even before my awakening, I was never someone who
dabbled with party drugs. Whenever someone at a party
would talk about cocaine, I'd just think of myself after a cup
of coffee. Over the years, so many people have called me the
Energizer Bunny. I was fast, fun, and full of energy no matter
the time of day. I already had way too much energy for people
to handle—the last thing I would do was *add* to that.

I lived in that state for a long time. Looking back, I wonder
how much of it was actually adrenaline from living in a
constant state of fight or flight because, when we've experienced trauma, the body can get stuck in that state, even when
there's no immediate threat. With what I had been through, it
was no wonder I was always buzzing. Although I'd done a lot
of healing, I still had a lot of energy. The difference was that,
then, it wasn't coming from survival—it's just who I am.

For the first twenty-five years of my life, I didn't feel called
to experiment with anything or "illegal" other than some

underage drinking. I had a deep fear of losing control of my mind. And honestly, I think that's one of the main reasons many people stay away from drugs and plant medicine. It's not always about the substance itself—it's the fear of what might surface when we're not the ones steering. For me, the fear ran deep: of going crazy, of not coming back, of remembering things I had worked hard to bury.

But, beneath all of that, it was really a fear of surrender. Control had always been my safety net. If I could plan, predict, or fix things, then maybe I wouldn't have to feel the chaos inside. But plant medicine doesn't let you think your way through it—it invites you into the unknown.

The first time I tried weed, it was a complete disaster. It didn't help me relax or open my mind; it sent me into a full-blown panic. For years, that "bad trip" caused me to write it off completely. I assumed weed just wasn't for me. But looking back now, I can see that my body wasn't ready. My nervous system was still stuck in survival, and my mind was doing everything it could to protect me from the memories trying to surface.

Years later, when a yoga teacher reintroduced me to marijuana in a safe, intentional way, the experience was completely different. My body was calmer, and for the first time, I felt clarity. Weed became a doorway, not a threat. It quieted the noise and allowed my higher self to come through. It reminded me of the stillness I feel when I meditate, that space where the mind softens and the truth rises. That's what ultimately led me to ayahuasca. I didn't go searching for it. I followed the clarity.

Ayahuasca is a powerful psychoactive plant medicine traditionally used by indigenous Amazonian communities for centuries. It is derived from a combination of two plants—Banisteriopsis caapi and Psychotria viridis. The active ingredient in ayahuasca is DMT (dimethyltryptamine), a potent hallucinogenic compound. The combination of these plants creates a brew with intense visionary effects.

When consumed in a ceremonial setting under the guidance of experienced practitioners, ayahuasca is believed to induce a heightened state of consciousness, leading to introspective insights, spiritual experiences, and potential healing. The brew is often considered a sacred teacher plant, revered for its ability to provide users with a profound journey of self-discovery and connection to the spiritual realms. I like to believe that I have a divinely guided relationship with plant medicine, but it is important to note that the use of ayahuasca should be approached with caution, respect, and supervision of knowledgeable individuals due to its powerful and potentially challenging effects.

In December 2022, before deciding we would leave my apartment in Santa Monica, Zack and I booked our second trip to visit my family in Boston. We were also talking about moving to Mexico for three months, where we would reset and save money until we decided where we wanted to live next.

One afternoon in meditation, I heard, *"You need to do ayahuasca before you move to Mexico. It's important. Go make a plan with Zack—talk to each other and make a plan."* Since beginning my microdose routine, I had come to feel comfortable with plant medicine, and I had built a solid amount of trust with myself. Since the call was coming from within, I felt good about it, so once I finished my meditation, I told Zack I needed to talk to him.

An hour later, Zack told me his friend was doing ayahuasca in LA in a few weeks and that he would ask if I could join. When he called his friend, though, he was told the ceremony was full. *No big deal*, I thought. *When I'm supposed to do it, it'll happen.* Then, no more than thirty minutes later, his friend called back and said someone else had just dropped out and that there was one spot open. It was mine if I wanted it. Well, of course I did! I got full-body chills and told him to sign me up right away. I was so excited, remembering that my friend's uncle had told me the plant medicine might help with my body flashbacks. Even the thought that they might go away was totally mind-blowing.

In anticipation of the ceremony, I scheduled a call with the practitioners and began the two-week cleansing diet, as it's recommended to adopt a mindful diet prior to the ceremony. Preparing for a plant medicine ceremony isn't just about what you eat; it's about how you care for your body, mind, and spirit leading up to it. I like to think of it as creating space physically, emotionally, and energetically for whatever needs to come through. That often looks like eating lighter, more natural foods; staying super hydrated; and cutting out things that cloud the system, like meat, dairy, caffeine, alcohol, and processed sugar. Even things like chocolate, anxiety, or sleep meds and sexual activity are usually avoided during this time because they can affect energetic clarity.

Mentally and emotionally, I already tended to stay away from anything that triggered me—no news, no intense media. Just peace, quiet, and space to reflect. The goal wasn't to be perfect; it was to be intentional. So I spent time getting clear on what I was calling in, what I was ready to let go of, and where I still needed healing. Spiritually, it was a time to sit with what was coming up—old wounds, forgiveness, resistance—and soften into it. This kind of preparation opens the door for a deeper experience. It wasn't about restriction—it was about devotion.

On the day of the ceremony, I sat on my mat in a circle with nineteen other people, filled with an overwhelming feeling that my life was about to change forever, though I didn't understand why or how. All of us were gathered there for the same purpose: to heal, to remember, and to return to ourselves. Before the medicine was served, we were given *hapé*—a sacred Amazonian tobacco used in ceremony to ground the body and clear the mind. I had never heard of it before. The moment it hit, a wave of intense nausea rushed through me. I could feel everything, myself, my body, my pain. It was overwhelming and clarifying all at once, like meeting the full weight of my emotional and energetic history head-on. Then came the ayahuasca.

As the medicine began to move through me, Grandmother Aya introduced herself with a gentle but commanding presence. She brought me straight into my sacral and solar plexus and said, *"Don't look there. You've seen enough."* With that, she began pulling thick, black energy from my body. I felt it releasing as she guided my attention upward. Then, she did something I'll never forget: she built what looked like the Great Wall of China in my brain. A barrier. A protection. She told me I didn't need to remember everything right now, and that it was time to stop looking for the pain. That I was safe.

She took me through my body, showing me ancestral wounds in the form of bugs that crawled through me. *"Kill them,"* she said. One by one, I crushed them with my hands, feeling the energy dissipate each time. She showed me my mother as a child and told me that what had happened to me wasn't her fault. *"Let go of the resentment,"* she said. And I did. I sobbed. And I burped—*a lot*. I didn't know then that burping was one of my body's ways of releasing energy. Every time I burped, I would burst into laughter. It was strange and beautiful.

After the heavy work was done, the ceremony took a lighter turn. I began to see my friends as animals—Zack was a dragon, flying through the sky. My close friend I had lived with at the penthouse appeared as a dolphin, smoking a joint while swimming through the ocean, laughing and saying, *"We're almost there—I can't wait to be with you."* And then, Grandmother said something that cracked me open: *"No more hiding. You are safe now. Share your story."*

When the ceremony ended, everyone in the room looked at me and said I looked like a completely different person. And they weren't wrong. I felt like I had undergone energetic surgery. Years of pain, shame, and trauma had been pulled out of me in a single night. I left that space feeling light, free, and deeply grateful. And somehow, as if to mark the shift, my body flashbacks were gone. Oh—and fun fact? I didn't puke even once.

What I learned was that losing control doesn't mean you're unsafe. Sometimes, doing so is the very thing that brings you back to yourself. I'm not here to convince anyone to try plant medicine. It's not for everyone, and timing matters. But if you ever feel called to it—not from pressure or hype, but from a quiet, deep place within—know that you don't have to *feel* fully "ready." You just have to be willing. Willing to be cracked open in service of your truth. Willing to meet parts of yourself you've never been allowed to meet before. Because sometimes what we're really afraid of isn't losing control, it's losing the identity we built to survive our pain.

From the moment I remembered what had happened to me as a child and spoke my truth, I had felt like I was wearing a scarlet letter. Although no one had said anything to make me feel this way, I felt like I was a walking reminder of the disgusting acts that were done to me. It wasn't until I worked through a lot of the stuck energies in my body that I was able to release that feeling. I had worked tirelessly on my mind, trying to change my thinking and reframe my experiences, but the weight of carrying something beyond my conscious mind kept me stuck in those old emotions. Plant medicine helped me release this and taught me how to work with my own energy body.

The old me would have been pissed, screaming inside, asking why I didn't do this sooner. But now, I felt a deeper peace. I knew everything was unfolding exactly as it should, and that it wasn't just about me. Real healing meant accepting every moment as it was, without needing to change it or rush the process.

Each time I have been called to plant medicine since, I have received what feels like an internal call from the plant through meditation. I have noticed a pattern in my waking life: Things seem to be fine on the surface in the physical world, but something feels off internally. I go through periods where I just don't feel like myself, where the many tools in my toolbox just don't seem to be doing the trick.

One spring morning at the beach with Zack, I felt plant medicine was calling me in meditation. I told him I felt I was supposed to do ayahuasca again soon, and being the good partner he is, he reminded me that I would be guided to it at the right time. A few days later, I found myself in conversation with a friend. We were connecting about one of her more recent experiences, which felt like she was experiencing another time and space in the present moment. One thing led to another, and she told me that she felt this was happening for her because she was doing bufo the following weekend.

Bufo isn't just a psychedelic; it's a deep, spiritual medicine. The 5-MeO-DMT compound, also known as bufo, comes from the secretion of the *Bufo alvarius* toad and is also something our bodies produce in small amounts during events like sleep, birth, orgasm, and death. These toads, found in the Sonoran desert, spend most of their lives underground and only come out during the rainy season. When harvested with care and respect, their secretion is collected and dried, then later smoked in ceremony. When experienced ceremonially, it can dissolve ego, clear out years of stored stress, and reconnect us to something far bigger than ourselves. For many, it feels like a direct return to Source.

When I told my friend I had been feeling called to ayahuasca again but didn't know a safe place nearby to join in a ceremony, she told me she was having a private ceremony at her home and invited me to join. I sat in meditation and asked my higher self, who gave me a very strong yes. These plants usually start working in your life as soon as you say yes to them. And what's wild is that the medicine doesn't stop working after the ceremony. It keeps unfolding for days or even weeks. That's why integration is so important. You're not just having a "trip," you're being invited into a deeper relationship with yourself.

Over the next few days, in preparation for the ceremony, I felt myself releasing and feeling into some of the things I had been avoiding looking at, specifically my time spent with my former life coach, Cassie, and the abuse I had endured. I worked with Zack to retrieve that part of myself and to forgive myself for having allowed that to happen to me, recognizing that I didn't know any better at that time. I slept a lot over that next week, more than I usually would, even taking naps during the day to allow myself to process whatever was trying to move through me. I started to feel a little lighter and clearer, but nowhere quite as clear as I would after this bufo ceremony.

Sunday morning came, and I had my intention ready for the ceremony: to release all of the judgment, shame, and resentment I still felt toward myself. Before the ceremony, I felt very calm and excited. Zack felt I would be visited by the dragon again, and I laughed, not really knowing what to expect. I had heard that bufo brings a lot of visuals and the connection with different realms. Well, that sure wasn't my experience!

When we arrived, the facilitators reminded us that although we had set our intentions for the ceremony, it was important to allow the plant to give us what we *needed*, not what we *wanted*. Having already experienced a few different plant medicines and a recent DMT trip, I was very open to this concept and didn't feel married to my intention. I trusted that whatever this medicine wanted to give me was exactly what I needed.

When it was finally my turn to receive the bufo, I went into the bedroom with the two medicine people, read the ceremonial prayer out loud, inhaled the medicine, and was laid down.

As excited as I had been, as soon as the bufo hit my lungs, my ego inner voice screamed, *"What the fuck was I thinking? I don't want to do this!"* I was overwhelmed by white light as the medicine man told me to open my mouth and gave me more of the bufo.

"I think I'm freaking out a bit," I told the medicine man.

Then, out of the white light, I heard God say, *"You must release this. Now is the time."*

The medicine assured me I was safe and that I could let it go, and I started releasing energy, screaming out the curses and energies inside of me until they were dispelled from my body. I told him I needed help getting it all out and directed him to take the energy out of my sacrals and solar plexus. Half conscious, I felt him begin to wipe it all out of my body, watching as a generational, ancestral curse was cleansed from my body. I began trauma shaking, crying my eyes out for my inner child, as I screamed, "Why did they do this to me?" I released as I fully re-experienced my childhood abuse throughout my whole system. I shot up and saw the look of horror on their faces as one of them said, "I bet you didn't expect to remove an ancient curse today." Then I laughed hysterically as I lay back down to release the rest. Half in shock and half in pride, I told the men how strong I was.

When it was finally over, I shot up and started laughing once again, feeling so good and so free. When I walked out of that room, I was a thousand times lighter. I had just experienced a full-blown exorcism. What a time to be alive!

I came to the understanding that I had broken a curse from my mother's lineage (my grandmother is first generation off the boat from Lebanon) that had been affecting my entire family. It was as if the pain, silence, and emotional suppression that had been passed down through generations had found a place to be seen and released through me, and I transmuted it for all of us. This wasn't just my healing; it was for every person who came before me and every one who would come after.

Many people, both seen and unseen, have helped me along the way, and for that I am grateful. Yet, most of all, I am grateful to myself for never giving up even when I felt completely helpless. There is nothing in this world that I am more proud of than looking at my past and facing all the pain I've endured. Doing so is the greatest gift we can give ourselves.

Regardless of what you have been through, I hope you, too, find the strength and courage within yourself to look your demons in the eye. I understand it may not feel like you can, but trust me—you are more than your feelings and your past, and there is nothing you cannot do. Beneath all the darkness you might be moving through is a light, quiet but steady and waiting to be found. It's not gone. It's guiding you, even now, toward exactly where you're meant to be. You are a powerful creator with the ability to heal yourself. Trust yourself.

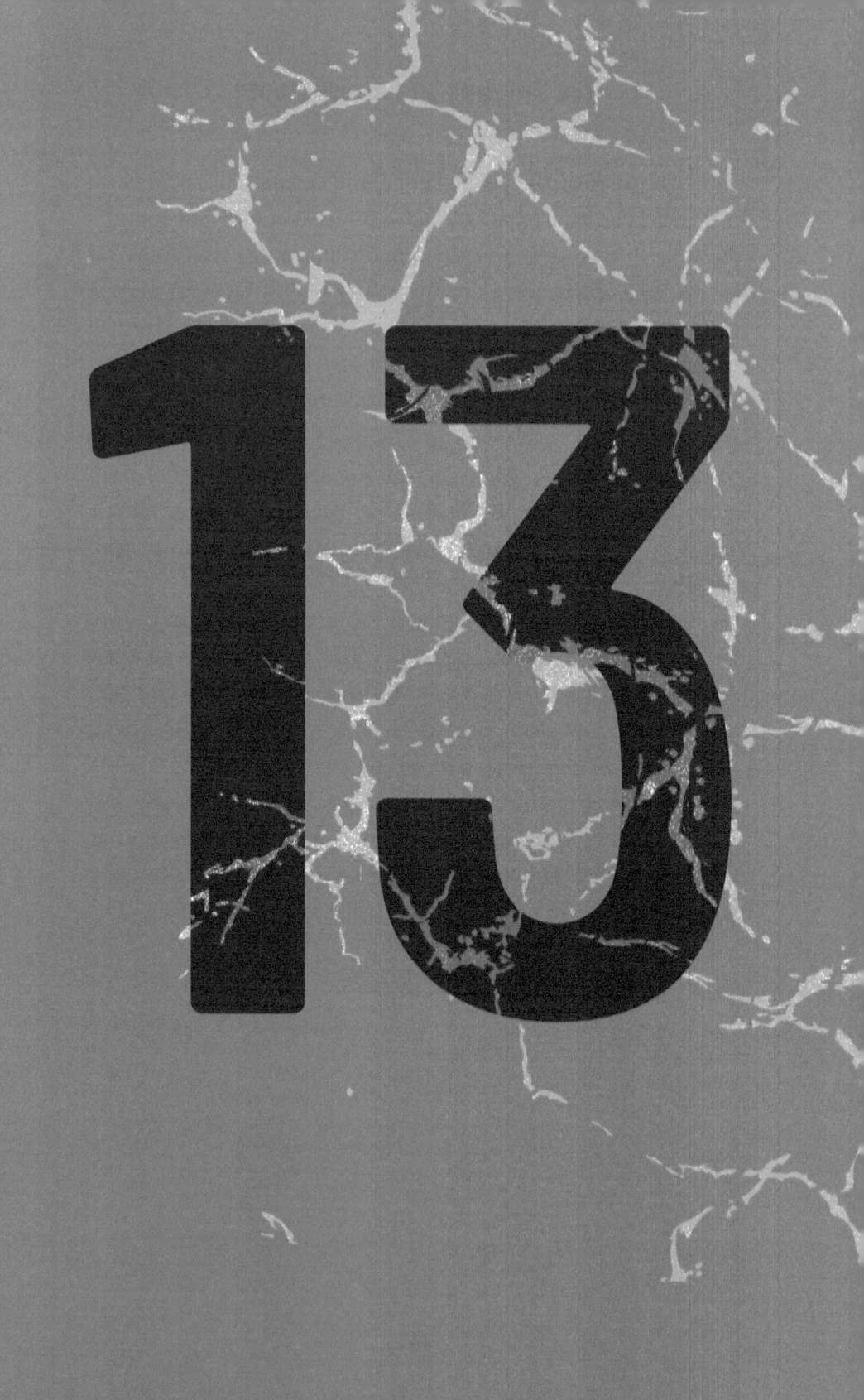

THE REAL WORK OF
COMING HOME

By the spring of 2023, Zack and I had packed up our bags, moved our stuff into storage, and set off to travel the world. Since I was leaving my job behind, Zack agreed to take financial care of me so that I could relax and heal from all I had been through on my own over the last five years. It had taken a few years, but I had finally done enough inner work to receive this type of support without any underlying fear, guilt, or anxiety. It felt different this time—not just because of *him* but because of *me*. Something had shifted. I was no longer letting my past dictate what I allowed myself to receive.

I knew I was attracting something new because I was being someone new. I was more open. More honest. More willing to be seen in my fear without letting it run the show. For the first time, I didn't feel like I owed anything in exchange. I was finally allowed to just be myself without feeling like I had to do anything "bad" to earn care or affection. It felt genuine.

Zack and I both knew it would be a stretch for him to take

on that kind of responsibility, just like it was a stretch for me to *receive* it. But we had the kind of relationship where we could talk about the hard things—money, triggers, fear, growth—so we leaned in anyway. The truth was, I no longer wanted to repeat old patterns. I wanted to build something new. And this—this kind of love, safety, and open communication—was exactly the kind of energy I had been calling in for years. I was extremely excited and grateful for this. Finally, the life of leisure I (or at least a part of me) had always desired!

Our first stop was to my favorite place in the entire world, Playa del Carmen, Mexico. Growing up, my mom was a travel agent, so every summer we took a trip to a resort there. I loved everything about it: the beach, the food, and the way I felt whenever I was there. I'd traveled to a lot of places around the world, but there was something undeniably magical about Mexico.

Within two weeks of being there, though, I was bored out of my mind. Part of the deal with Zack was that I would continue working toward my purpose in life while he took care of me, and I was driving him crazy, ready to get to work again and be of service in the world. I always knew I wanted to write a book and tell my story, but I had tried many times before and always struggled to find the words I wanted to say. I can't even begin to tell you how many hours I spent going through journals and Word documents, trying to piece together everything. I knew it was something I was supposed to do, but I couldn't understand why I always seemed to be met with such resistance. Looking back now, it's crystal clear that there were things I still had to learn and experience before sharing the most intimate details of my life with the world.

One day, I received a message from someone who helped people write their books. (Coincidence? We know those don't exist!) This felt like a sign, so I immediately set up a call to discuss further. The pricing was out of my budget, but it felt like now was the perfect time for me to write a book. When I met with the book doula, Amanda, she felt like the perfect fit.

Although it was challenging when Amanda and I started working together, things started flowing through me. For as long as I could remember, every accomplishment in my life had come from a place of stress. I had always been motivated by "just getting it done," getting from point A to point B. I learned that, just like the healing process, the writing process is also not linear. So many other things I had done in my life were through my own force and will. But this was different.

I wanted this process to be quick and easy. I wanted it just to be done. But my tendency to push through instead of sitting with my feelings was challenged with every writing session I had. Parts of me wanted to sit down and type it all out straight away, but there were many moments when I sat and stared blankly at the computer screen, too overwhelmed with emotion to continue.

With every word I wrote, I was met and greeted by the feelings that were still lingering in my body. I was challenged not only to face my past again but to see it in a different light while viscerally reliving all that I had endured. If I wrote something that I had not fully emotionally processed yet, my body would rob my mind of its ability to think. This forced me to sit with myself over and over again and truly process the things I had been through—not only from childhood but also everything since. Each time I wrote, I wanted to write more, but I couldn't always do that.

The process challenged everything I believed about myself. Initially, it made me feel angry and frustrated with myself. Sometimes, I felt paralyzed and confused. Why wouldn't more come out? I already knew what had happened—I had lived it! I had survived! But that wasn't the point. My internal bully couldn't be the one guiding this project. Instead, I allowed myself to be guided each time to sit and process my feelings about what I was writing. It was both a beautiful and painful experience.

Eventually, I reached a place of acceptance in regards to my writing. Instead of willing my way through like I tended to, I needed to give myself a break. It wasn't up to me when everything would be done. Some divine orchestration that I couldn't quite see was occurring, and I was going to lean into it.

After all the work I had done, I knew that logically grasping the things that happen to us is one thing but the way through is by *feeling*. The awareness of this had taught me to truly feel my feelings without attaching stories to them—which can be difficult when writing a book. Sitting by the ocean or on my rooftop, I would place my hand on my heart and tell my mind I didn't need any visuals and to just let my body feel. I experienced so many realizations, changes, and *aha* moments throughout this period, and each one brought with it a new level of awareness and self-connection. I also experienced a deep inner knowing that it all needed to come not from me but through me. It had to come from my higher self and a higher perspective.

There is something powerful about putting our stories

on paper and letting them be seen, first by ourselves and then maybe by others. It's a kind of safe liberation, a way to free what's been stuck without having to scream it from a rooftop. Many times during the process, I found myself pouring out my heavy, unprocessed feelings, and although the things I have endured in my life have caused me immense pain, it was never about that for me.

Writing this book was about more than just telling my story. It was also about processing whatever I had left to feel from my past and transmuting my story in a way that would help empower people to heal and know they are not alone. To know that there *is* light at the end of the tunnel, and though there continue to be hard days, the pain lessens over time once we start feeling the emotions we've carried from the past.

When I began writing, I had already processed a lot, but the more severe the trauma, the more there is to get at. If our bodies are like pools of water, I had scrubbed up the muck from the bottom, but there were still leaves and residue I needed to reach at the top. The whole time, Zack really encouraged me to talk to him about what was coming up. We had already built such a deep connection, but this brought a new level of intimacy to our relationship. I had to learn to open up even more, to him as well as other friends who were there to hold space for me. It was a very healing experience.

One day, sweating in the Mexican heat, I was having a deep conversation with my brother via text message. We were talking about childhood and whatnot, and now he mentioned he wanted to do ayahuasca. I told him that I also wanted to do it again. No more than thirty seconds later, a woman I had done a kambo ceremony with messaged me saying she would be holding an all-women's ayahuasca and kambo retreat in two weeks.

My brain went spinning. Was I supposed to do ayahuasca again? I had an amazing experience the first time, and I had talked about wanting to do it again, but Zack had seen many clients abuse plant medicine, and we both wanted to make sure that whenever I did it again, it would be because I was genuinely guided to do so. It's yet another thing I appreciate about my partner.

I kept the thought in the back of my mind, talking to both Zack and Gina about it as well as meditating on it. When my meditation gave me a solid yes, I submitted my deposit and started the preparatory diet once again. Ten days later, off I went to the jungle to throw up in a bucket with six other women.

This ceremony would be my first experience taking two plant medicines in one day, as it also included kambo, a traditional healing ritual that has been used for centuries by Amazonian tribes for physical and spiritual healing. Secretion from the giant monkey frog, which contains bioactive peptides believed to detoxify the body, boost the immune system, and improve mental clarity, is applied to small burns on the skin. The process can cause intense reactions like vomiting and sweating, which are considered part of the cleansing.

I had set my intention for the medicine to align me with my highest timeline, and my second journey with Grandmother Ayahuasca was completely different from the first, though it was just as sacred. As before, she told me I didn't need to look at my pain—I had already seen enough.

She reminded me that she would take it from me. No more suffering for the sake of healing. Just surrender.

Then, she introduced me to my future daughter. She told me her name and that she wanted to be just like me. That she chose me so she could experience the childhood I never had. I had never purged in any ceremony before, but in that moment, I did. It felt like entire lifetimes were leaving my body.

After that release, I was guided to look up, where I saw parts of myself trapped in the past—old versions of me, frozen in time. She taught me how to retrieve them and call those parts back into my body. Fully integrated and whole, I wouldn't be creating from fractured places anymore. She told me this was my first shamanic initiation and that I would guide others through the same. After that, I rested. I watched the music and the messages about the collective that poured in like waves. I left the ceremony not just healed, but as someone who remembered who the fuck she was. I felt whole, happy, ready.

A few weeks later, in June, I finished the rough draft of this book. My first round of work was done. I felt proud. I was ready to move forward—until I wasn't. Every time I sat down to work on the next drafts, I felt blocked. No energy. No clarity. Just a full-body *no*. So I stopped pushing. I leaned into divine timing and trusted it. Months passed. Still no.

In December of 2023, Zack and I headed to Boston for Christmas. We both agreed there was something magical about being around my family, especially for us. We were so used to giving our energy to both our lives and careers that going back to where we felt loved and taken care of seemed to breathe life back into us. Returning home this time, I felt like a completely different person, a more grounded version of myself. I was excited to see how it played out.

The night Zack and I arrived at my parents' house, I felt a strong surge of energy despite how late it was and what a long day of travel it had been. I realized that my family was giving me energy without wanting anything in return, something I had never felt in my body before. For the first time, I was *feeling* love. Not because I hadn't been loved before, but because I had spent years not being present in my body, with myself or with others. I had had a happy home, but this was the first time in my life I had felt safe enough to be present and receive love from my loved ones.

This visit coincided with the seventh anniversary of my initial remembrance of the trauma. Previously, it was a big trigger date that had me feeling emotionally and physically consumed by the past. I had looked at it as my "rebirthday," a date I always held in the back of my mind that marked when my entire life changed, when I met myself and truth. Although the day brought a lot of pain, I found solace in the fact that as each year passed, I found myself in a better place—mentally, emotionally, physically, and spiritually—than I had been the previous year.

As the date approached, I sat in meditation and had what felt like a big realization. I had heard about life happening in seven-year cycles, unfolding as each seven-year increment came to represent different stages of development within our minds and bodies. Spiritually and psychologically, I was at the end of the seventh year of my awakening journey. I could feel the changes within me and the change that was about to come.

That year, when January 3 rolled around, instead of feeling

dread, I was genuinely full of hope, excited in my body for what my next chapter was going to look like. For the first time since my awakening, that perpetually lingering feeling that there was still "more" for me to uncover about my past wasn't present at all. I had an amazing time with my friends and family, and my heart was filled with gratitude for myself that all the hard work I had done in the past seven years had officially paid off. I could feel and see it in my everyday reality.

I couldn't remember ever feeling more seen, heard, accepted, and loved in my entire life than I did during that trip to my parents'. My family had always been accepting and loving, but my self-perception had affected my perception of others for so long. After all of the years of dismissing my family's reassurances that I wasn't crazy and no one thought I was, I finally felt safe to be all the versions of myself, confident in myself and my knowledge that I was very much a sane, happy, and healthy person. And that truth was reflected by everyone around me.

They say that you get back what you put out there. Well, I have seen both sides of the coin. When I am feeling crazy and tell myself that, then that's the energy I receive. When I am secure, grounded, and happy, then that's what comes my way. The Universe doesn't care what you want; it only acts on what you believe. This was the catalyst that helped me feel safe enough to change.

It may have taken thirty-two years, but hey! I still got there! And it's one of the greatest blessings I could ever ask for. I didn't need anyone else to change; it was me who changed— how I acted, how I showed up, and how I felt about myself. It was a very important lesson for me, and I hope it serves as a reminder to you, too, that we are in charge of ourselves. How we show up is what we attract, and I had finally reached a place where I truly loved and accepted myself. What followed was the world reflecting that back to me—not in some magical, instant way, but in the quiet, consistent way life does when we stop abandoning ourselves.

For the past seven years, I had spent a lot of time wondering why my abusers did what they did to me, and who could be so sick to want to hurt a child—perfectly rational thoughts for those of us who couldn't fathom hurting someone else, never mind a child. But sometimes we have to look deeper than we think to discover why people do what they do. It wasn't until I was back in Mexico attending a family constellation therapy session Gina had introduced me to that the pieces clicked into logical place.

Imagine your family as a puzzle, where each member is a piece that fits together to create the whole picture. In family constellation therapy, the client works with a therapist to explore the relationships and dynamics within their family. Physical objects like paper or tokens may be used to represent family members, and the objects are arranged to create a visual representation of the family system. The practitioner may even channel a family member's energy, using these tools to help identify patterns, connections, and unresolved issues within the family.

If there's tension or conflict between family members, for instance, the practitioner might notice how the pieces are arranged and work with the client to find ways to improve the relationships, repositioning the objects or adding new ones to create a more balanced and harmonious family "picture."

This process can help the client gain insights, heal emotional wounds, and find resolutions to conflict. Overall, it's a creative and symbolic way to explore family relationships and find ways to make them healthier and more supportive.

During my Zoom session, I was lying comfortably in bed as the practitioner, Tammy, channeled the energy of each of my relatives. As she did, I was able not just to see but also to feel where the abuse started and why it had been projected onto me. It confirmed that the people who had hurt me had also been hurt by someone in a position of power and that their inability to cope with what they had experienced caused them to desire to take power over innocent children, in a sense, reenacting what happened to them. It wasn't about sexual desire; it was about having power and control, which had been taken from them in the past.

This same dynamic can be seen by men who were bullied or ostracized by girls only to become adults who hate women. How many times have we heard about the "weird kid" who grew up to be the guy who mistreats women? No one wakes up one day and just decides to commit heinous acts; all of these brutal traumas stem from somewhere. As fucked up as it is, it is sometimes the psyche's way of dealing with one's own untreated trauma.

This is why it is so important to look at what has happened to us and actively make the decision to heal or move forward from it. Hurt people hurt people, but we all have a choice in this life. Do I think my abusers consciously chose to become pedophiles? No, I don't. I think the shame, secrecy, and unspoken pain they were carrying shaped them in ways they didn't fully understand. That doesn't excuse the harm. It doesn't make it okay. But it does reveal something about how trauma festers when it's never named and never faced. Sometimes people become the thing they were most afraid of—or the thing that was done to them—because they never found a way to break the cycle.

When I came to this realization after family constellation therapy, I had another sigh of relief. The anger dissipated, and I felt like I could breathe. For so long, I had carried the feeling that it had been my fault. That I should have spoken up, or that maybe if I had looked different, it wouldn't have happened to me. The truth of the situation was that none of it was even in my control. My abusers' desire for power and control over anyone and anything would still have caused them to harm me. Nothing I could have done as a child would have made a difference.

Although these were still hard truths to swallow, it was freeing to know that I truly couldn't have changed anything about the past. There was nothing I could have done differently, and now I got to actively choose to step into my power every day and create the life I wanted for myself.

I applaud my younger self for being so incredibly intelligent about how to cope with keeping such heavy trauma hidden from myself and everyone around me. Because, if we're being real, many people might choose drugs and alcohol to cope with these things—and I honestly can't blame them. As a trauma survivor, one of the first things I said to my therapist was how I really understood why people do drugs. Nothing feels worse than being uncomfortable in your own skin because of something that was done to you against your will. Yet, as I zoom out and look at my journey prior to the remembrance of my trauma, I see how many of the "habits" I developed as trauma responses are things our society celebrates, like overexercising and overworking.

Becoming athletic at the age of fourteen and continuing ever since made me feel confident, strong, and in control, and I loved how I felt after pushing myself to the limit. I was the one making my heart race, not the stress or anxiety. I even made a career out of exercising!

This portion of my life, although it served me greatly, was not the ultimate answer. The habits were taken to an unhealthy level, and the pattern was very challenging to unlearn. I over-exercised in the name of healing, going to yoga in the morning and the gym for two to four hours at night. Granted, I had plenty of energy because I was detached from my body and heavily medicated, but I was abusing my own body. Since the abuse was no longer occurring, I became my own abuser.

I played this scenario out for a very long time before I was able to recognize and accept what I was doing to myself, making excuses about it being the "only thing that helped me" or something I needed to feel okay. I was so stuck in my own perspective of it that I was in complete denial about what was going on. Regardless of which method of self-harm a person is doing, they are searching for the same thing: the feeling of control and safety. If I'm doing this to myself, then no one else can.

But we only ever create the illusion of control. No one has control over what happens, but the desire to *feel* in control remains until we finally process the things that happen to us. Once I learned that every time I thought *I feel fat* and what I really meant was I felt shame and didn't understand where it was coming from, I was able to practice sitting with and feeling the shame without assigning it a story or rational explanation.

I now know I don't need a reason to feel anything. I don't need to mentally revisit every story to release what's stuck. Just feeling the emotion in my body without needing to explain or justify it is enough. If I could go back, I probably could have saved myself from constantly reliving my visual memories. But I wasn't there yet; I didn't know that was an option. Back then, there was a distinct part of me that *needed* me to suffer with her. She held the pain, and suffering was her proof that what happened mattered.

When you carry traumatic memories in silence for so long, your nervous system gets tangled in them. There's often an unconscious attachment to the pain, not because you're weak or broken, but because some part of you doesn't trust the pain will be honored unless it's constantly present. That part wants the world to finally acknowledge: *This happened. This hurt. And I'm still here.*

Up until recently, these topics haven't been very openly discussed, and we weren't taught the proper coping or prevention skills. But, perhaps due to the shame it carries, the collective shadow of abuse has grown to a point where it has no choice but to show itself. Letting go doesn't mean forgetting. It means releasing the emotional charge so you can hold your story without being crushed by it. I urge you to give yourself permission to let go of the visuals that are causing you pain. Feel through the emotions, knowing that there is relief on the other side.

THE MEDICINE WAS
ALWAYS ME

I see my energy like an infinity loop—constantly flowing, expanding, returning. The more present I am, the more embodied I feel. And the more embodied I feel, the more life opens up for me, without force and without effort. It's wild; the more I practice being here now, the more I feel my own energy. I've started craving it. I used to always reach outside of myself, but now, I want to be with myself. The more I sit with me, the more in tune I become. I can feel my energy growing, stretching, dancing in front of me. It's alive. It's mine. And it's always been waiting for me to come home to it.

I've truly gotten to a place where I've completely surrendered, knowing that everything is happening as it should. I feel calm now, whereas I used to spend my days making my heart race so I could feel in control and match the severe trauma my body was carrying. My time is utilized towards regulation and relaxation, and I feel open and receptive because of the calm and peace.

A significant progression is reaching a place where we no longer project our trauma onto others. Many people who were meant to be corrective experiences along my journey couldn't be received as such yet because I was still so drenched in my trauma patterns. I am grateful for these people who understood me and helped me along the way so I could reach this point. I now trust myself enough to tell the difference between when it's my trauma and when it's my intuition speaking to me. I also no longer manifest from those lower, traumatized parts of my psyche.

Trauma and intuition can both show up as gut feelings, but they come from very different places. Learning to tell the difference between them has been one of the most important parts of my healing. Trauma is reactive. It speaks from fear and past pain, and it often feels urgent, loud, or panicked. It's trying to protect you from something you've already lived through.

Intuition, on the other hand, is calm and steady. Even when it's guiding you away from something, it does so with clarity, not anxiety. It's a quiet knowing that doesn't argue or justify itself. For example, I might get invited somewhere and immediately feel like I don't want to go. If that feeling is rooted in trauma, it usually comes with a flood of anxious thoughts: *What if they judge me? What if I'm not safe? What if I don't belong?* But if it's my intuition, the message is much simpler: *Not this one. You need rest. Something's off.* The more I've slowed down and practiced listening, the easier it's become to tell which voice is speaking. One helps me hide. The other helps me return to myself.

Another important takeaway is that I no longer feel shame around the multiple voices I hear in my mind. I understand deeply that they are not a mental disorder but a brilliant coping strategy I've utilized in moments when I had no choice but to survive. Now, all of the parts inside of me are working for me, not against me. I'm so much less fragmented than I thought.

I used to feel a lot of guilt and shame about how speaking about my trauma triggered others. I stewed in these feelings for some time, feeling bad about how I thought I made others feel, but the truth is that expressing our truth is what helps others release their own shame. Even if I may "trigger" some people, I know that others are helped when we give them a space to heal and feel safe as they face their own experiences.

Over and over again, I had to lean into feeling my "why"— why I wrote this book, why I felt called to share my story. Every time I did, I visualized the younger me who needed this when she first recalled her trauma and all the other people out there who have experienced and will experience the same thing. It's a scary place to be, having no tangible evidence of something so intense besides your own mind and body. But my trust that the body knows more than we could ever imagine is why I wanted to share this with the world. Psychology may tell us one thing, but we can always trust our bodies and intuition. Only you know your truth; never let anyone else convince you otherwise.

Reflecting on the "whys" behind my journey, there were two things in particular I wanted for certain: a better relationship with myself and a relationship with my family and friends that felt good and healthy. For so long, I had kept my distance, feeling like an outsider while the people I loved were waiting for me to come back around. When I uprooted my life to California, I knew it had been exactly what I needed at the time. Someone once told me, "You can't heal where you were hurt," and it has always resonated deeply with me. As much as I missed my family and harbored subconscious guilt for being far away, the weight of my body's memories was almost too much to bear. Constantly reliving the past in my body and speaking it out loud only made the pain worse for me and everyone around me.

When we heal from the bad things that have happened to us, our loved ones heal too because, when trauma happens to one person, it also happens to the people they love. My family and friends were just as desperate to help me through my pain, but, of course, it was my job to figure out how to transmute it. I can proudly say that's what I did.

The Universe is always whispering to us, and it's our job to slow down, take space, be present, and listen. It is not easy to trust the trajectory of life. It's much easier to try to will your way forward by putting your energy toward accomplishing goals. I hope my story helps you understand that your true power lies in your ability to surrender, trust, and take inspired action to reach levels you can't yet imagine. As you listen to yourself, even if that means doing things that may not make sense to you in the moment, every action you take will be supported by the Universe as you learn to surrender, trust, and co-create. Have patience with yourself, forgive yourself, and always know you can do anything and everything you set your mind to.

Looking back, I can't always believe what I've lived through. And what amazes me even more is that despite everything, I kept following my inner guidance even when it made no logical sense. That's the thing about intuition: it rarely speaks the language of logic. But it knows. And every time I choose to listen, even through fear or doubt, it carves a path forward. If you've survived hard things, a part of you already knows the way. You don't need to see the whole map to take the next step. You just need to trust the pull.

Eventually, I reached the level of self-trust where I stopped following my inner guidance out of desperation or fear and started following it simply because I *wanted* to. I realized I didn't need to be in a constant state of healing to be whole. I already *was* whole. The real healing is in how I live day to day—feeling what comes up, letting it move through, and then grounding back into the present moment. That's where freedom lives. The more that I am here now, the more embodied I am, and the more magic unfolds in my life without me even trying.

As soon as Zack and I got back home, I felt the call to sit with Grandmother Aya again. I thought maybe this was the clarity I needed for the book. Within days of paying the deposit for the February ceremony, I got a call from my parents. My grandmother, Sito, was dying. I needed to come back to say goodbye.

We were always close with Sito and even lived with her for a time. Sito was the mother of my abusers, and I loved her deeply. She developed dementia around the time I began having my first memories. We always said that was a gift because if she had known what happened to me, she would've burned the whole house down.

For eight years, I had carried the weight of not telling her. I had thought about it and talked about it with friends, but something had always told me it wasn't the time. Until it was.

The day after the phone call, I got on a plane. I went to see Sito as soon as I arrived. And as I sat beside her, I took her hand and told her the truth. I told her why her sons hadn't been around. I told her what they did. And I told her I was okay. I told her it was safe to go. That Gidu, her husband, was waiting for her. That she didn't have to carry any of this into the afterlife. That I was free, and she could be too.

The doctors had said it was the end and she could go at any moment—she hadn't eaten, hadn't drunk water in days. Her body was shutting down. I cried harder than I had in years and said my goodbyes. But I needed her to know the truth before she left.

The next day, I walked into her room again and saw her sitting up—smiling, laughing, eating, drinking—like nothing had happened. Had I somehow brought my grandmother back to life? We played music and laughed and danced like we used to. She must've missed her exit, we all decided.

I got two more weeks with her—two of the most sacred weeks of my life. A few days before she passed, I sat in a room with my parents. They said, "Well, at least she didn't know what happened to you." And I told them the truth, that I *did* tell her. I told them I felt that knowing would free her, not burden her. That I did it with love. That I did it for her too. They took it in. They understood.

We had the most beautiful funeral I'd ever seen. She looked radiant and peaceful, like she knew everything now and was finally resting. She passed away on February 17, 2025. The day of her funeral was the same day I was supposed to sit in that ayahuasca ceremony. Of course it was. It felt like divine orchestration. Like the ceremony had already happened—in real life. I had closed a chapter of my maternal line. I had broken a cycle. I had spoken the truth. And in doing so, I helped release her soul and mine. This *was* the ceremony. And it changed everything.

Zack and I returned to Mexico, and I let myself grieve. I watched a lot of TV. There were mornings I didn't want to get out of bed—so I didn't. I listened to my body. There weren't many tears, but there was a deep heaviness I trusted would move when it was ready. By then, I had learned to trust my process. I didn't need to force myself into a better place. I just needed to let myself *be*.

A few months passed. I danced a lot. I went to samba class, moving energy the way my body asked me to. I worked out—not to change anything, but to stay connected to myself. Movement became my medicine. Silence too. And then, the call came again. Grandmother Aya was reaching out—this time for a private ceremony.

I sat with myself for a while, waiting for the right intention to come through. I knew I was being called back in, but I didn't want to rush. With time, I started to see what was really in the way—I was still afraid of being fully seen. From the outside, I looked open, vulnerable, even brave. But there was a shield over me, subtle but strong, keeping me just out of reach of my full potential.

When I saw it clearly, I got honest. And I set my intention: "I am ready to let love take up the space that trauma once held. I trust that I've seen enough—and now, I welcome clarity, peace, and purpose as I step fully into the life I was always meant to live. Guide me gently forward and help me feel safe in the becoming."

The morning of the ceremony, I sat on the toilet and noticed I had gotten my period. I knew it was close, but I track my cycle—this wasn't supposed to happen yet. I messaged the shaman, and she said she already knew. Spirit had told her days ago that I'd be bleeding. She told me that when a woman is on her moon during ceremony, the medicine becomes even more powerful.

That night, we went deep into the jungle. Before the ceremony began, the shaman taped an herb and a crystal over my belly button to help contain the energy. The first blow of hapé hit—and I was already crying. I heard Grandmother Aya immediately: *"You're doing such a good job. I'm so proud of you."*

Before the first glass, we pulled cards from an oracle deck. I withdrew one that said, "I let go of my armor." Of course I did. I drank my first cup and immediately heard, *"Life is messy, but there's beauty in all of it."* The energy started moving through me in waves. I kept hearing, *"Surrender. You are safe."*

With the second cup, my future child flew down to meet me. She showed up as a dolphin, smiling in my face. She told me it wasn't her time yet but that she was always with me—and she couldn't wait to meet me when the time was right. She showed me and Zack as her whale parents, steady and strong.

Then my grandmother Sito appeared. She told me she missed me and loved me. That I should tell my mother she did an incredible job taking care of her. That there was no need to miss her—because she was still here. She apologized for everything I went through. Told me how strong I was. She said that soon I would understand. And then came the flood.

Spiritual gifts poured in—messages from plants, goddesses, and ancient energies. I was being given visions, insights, new sensitivities—clairvoyance, clairaudience, clairsentience. And my whole body was receiving. My mouth opened to speak what was arriving. Then, everything stopped.

I heard a voice ask, *"Do you choose the gifts, or do you choose*

God?" Without hesitation, I said, "I choose God." And then God came to me. He said, *"Because you chose Me, you can keep everything that was given to you."*

He held my inner child in a magical place. Whispered truths into my soul. Gave me assignments for this lifetime. Told me I was doing a great job—and that now He was going to show me *everything.* He showed me that all is one. That I had chosen every piece of my life before I came here—even my name, Gabriella, *God is my strength.*

He showed me how the transmutation of pain creates medicine. That my story would help others *feel.* That's the point of life—to feel it all. The one thing we lose when we die is our ability to feel. And so, while we're here, we're meant to feel it *fully.*

I also received truths I wasn't ready for—truths I didn't want to be true. Every time things got heavier, I was tested. I was offered paths, temptations, power, but every time, I chose God. I chose the light again and again.

By the time we finished at around 4 a.m., I was empty. Full. Elated. Wrecked. Reborn.

I left that day feeling whole, complete, grounded in my truth. There was a new kind of gratitude in me—for *everything.* The good, the bad, the lessons, all of it. For the first time, I truly understood the purpose behind my pain.

I wasn't carrying the emotional weight anymore—I was carrying the *purpose.* The *medicine.* My story *is* the medicine. It exists to help others see what they haven't been able to see.

Turn inward. Because the answers aren't out there. They're inside. Only you can unlock them.

RESOURCES

Healing Back Pain by John Sarno

Trauma and Recovery by Judith Herman

The Power of Positive Thinking by Norman Vincent Peale

Why Can't I Meditate? by Nigel Wellings

The Body Keeps the Score: Brain, Mind, and Body in the Healing of Trauma by Bessel van der Kolk, M.D.

How to Do the Work: Recognize Your Patterns, Heal from Your Past, and Create Your Self by Dr. Nicole LePera

Judgment Detox: Release the Beliefs That Hold You Back from Living a Better Life by Gabrielle Bernstein

The Big Leap: Conquer Your Hidden Fear and Take Life to the Next Level by Gay Hendricks

Healing the Fragmented Selves of Trauma Survivors: Overcoming Internal Self-Alienation by Janina Fisher, Ph.D.

ACKNOWLEDGEMENTS

To Zack—thank you for being my unwavering support. For loving me through every version of myself, encouraging me when I doubted everything, and standing beside me on every level—emotionally, spiritually, and practically—as I birthed this book and rebuilt my life. I love you with all my heart.

To my family—especially my parents and the Cacciatore side—thank you for meeting me with love, support, and open arms when I finally spoke my truth. Your acceptance gave me the safety to keep going. I feel deeply grateful to have been born into a family that not only stood by me but chose to walk this healing path with me. Thank you for loving the version of me that was in pain and for embracing the one who has risen from it.

To Amanda, my book doula—thank you for showing up as the exact person I needed to help bring this to life. Your patience, insight, and steady presence helped me shape something that once felt impossible. I'm so grateful the Universe guided me to you.

To everyone I've met along the way—my friends, healers,

soul connections, and every person who touched my rawness and let me be exactly who I was—thank you. Your presence, encouragement, and belief in me mattered more than you'll ever know.

To the Universe—thank you for every nudge, synchronicity, plot twist, and miracle. You never stopped guiding me—even when I couldn't see it.

And lastly, to myself—thank you for not giving up. For facing the fire, telling the truth, doing the work, and choosing life over and over again. I'm proud of you. I love you. You did it.

ABOUT THE AUTHOR

Gabriella Cacciatore is a trauma-informed coach, writer, and spiritual guide who helps others reconnect with their bodies, rebuild self-trust, and remember their truth. After surviving complex childhood trauma and experiencing a life-changing spiritual awakening, she committed to healing from the inside out. Her work weaves together somatic healing, emotional integration, and nervous system regulation. Through her writing, she offers others the permission to feel deeply, speak honestly, and come home to themselves. *Unbroken* is her debut book—a love letter to the parts of us that never stopped trying to survive. She currently lives in Mexico with her partner and their two cats and spends her time in community—working out, dancing, and playing pickleball. You can reach her on Instagram @gabcacc or by email at gabcacciatore@gmail.com or learn more by going to awakenvillagepress.com/gabriella-cacciatore.

www.ingramcontent.com/pod-product-compliance
Lightning Source LLC
Chambersburg PA
CBHW031502120626
46545CB00005B/1708